100
DISNEY
ADVENTURES
OF A LIFETIME

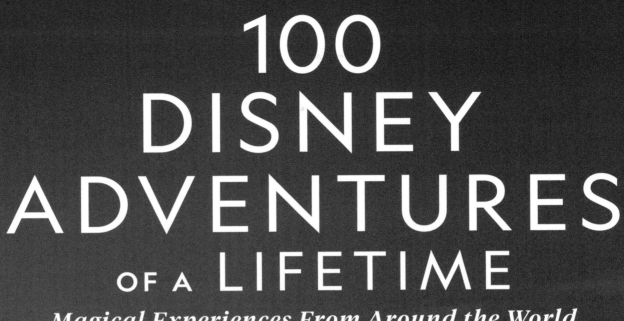

100
DISNEY
ADVENTURES
OF A LIFETIME

Magical Experiences From Around the World

MARCY CARRIKER SMOTHERS

FOREWORD BY JOE ROHDE

NATIONAL
GEOGRAPHIC

WASHINGTON, D.C.

CONTENTS

PAGES 2-3: Disney's Monorail takes you between the Magic Kingdom, EPCOT, and various Walt Disney World resorts.

OPPOSITE: Conquer the mountains of Disney (page 166), including Big Thunder Mountain Railroad, the wildest ride in the West.

FOREWORD

As a young designer, I had the privilege of knowing some of Walt Disney's original Imagineers, whose love of travel and exploration led to iconic experiences for Disney theme park guests. Disney Legend Herb Ryman, who drew the first designs for Disneyland, talked about standing amid the ruins of Angkor Wat as a young man. Disney Legend Marc Davis, famous for everything from *Snow White and the Seven Dwarfs* (1937) to the Pirates of the Caribbean attraction, had a home so crammed with artifacts from Papua New Guinea and Africa that you had to walk sideways to get to the flat files stacked with his field sketches of tribal art and culture. I learned from them that the imagination is fed not only from within but also by the choice to step out into the world and see what might happen.

My own Imagineering career eventually led me and my teams on our own adventures researching Disney's Animal Kingdom. From camping in the Serengeti to caving in Thailand to exploring Maya ruins in the Yucatán and even participating in scientific research expeditions in the Himalaya, we were able to absorb and bring back the essence of adventure, distilled into design, for others to enjoy. That's what Disney offers everyone: through adventures of every size and style, a distillation of the essence of experience brewed to perfection in the cauldron of the imagination, an invitation to one and all.

But it doesn't stop there. The world is filled with adventurous lives that got their start from a Disney experience, whether a conservation biologist who went to Disney's Animal Kingdom as a kid; an innovative engineer who was fascinated by the technology of *Star Wars: Galaxy's Edge;* a tourist inspired to explore Hawai'i deeply because of a visit to Aulani, A Disney Resort & Spa; or a child who gained confidence by taking their first ride on Big Thunder

Mountain Railroad. Adventure begets adventure. The tiniest first step can lead to an endless lifelong journey.

So, step out, make a choice, and see what happens. That is what adventure means, literally, from the original Latin *adventurus*, meaning "about to happen." This book is a compendium of adventures, some full of exoticism and thrills, others closer to home and smaller in scale, all bringing a chance for something to happen. All you have to do is choose an adventure and go. ■

—Joe Rohde
Former Imagineer

Inspired by his research expeditions, Joe Rohde paints a feature on a rock in Disney's Animal Kingdom Theme Park.

INTRODUCTION

Walt Disney came to California in July 1923 with a suitcase and a dream.

At 21 years old, his Laugh-O-gram Films studio (where he made a series of seven modernized versions of fairy tales) in Kansas City, Missouri, went bankrupt when the distributor defaulted on his payments. His big brother Roy suggested, "Kid, I think you should get out of there."

Walt, a lifelong railroad enthusiast, heeded Roy's advice and booked a train ticket west. Although his cash and personal possessions were limited, his characteristic optimism was abundant: "It was a big day, the day I got on that Santa Fe Limited, and came to Hollywood. I was just free and happy you know?"

When Walt arrived, he rented a room from his uncle Robert and charted a change in course: "I was fed up with cartoons. My ambition at that time was to be a director." When his silver screen job didn't materialize, Walt returned to what he knew. Renting Uncle Robert's garage, he hand-built an animation stand using scrap lumber and established his "new cartoon studio." It was originally known as the Disney Brothers Cartoon Studio; later, Roy—an equal partner—removed any reference to himself, renaming the brothers' joint venture the Walt Disney Studio.

In October 1923, Walt was offered a contract for the *Alice Comedies* (a live-action little girl in an animated world), an event so historic, Walt Disney Archives founder and Disney Legend Dave Smith describes the original document as the "most important in the history of The Walt Disney Company." Why? Because this is the start of Disney as we know it!

National Geographic, founded in 1888 by a group of elite scholars, explorers, and scientists, joined the Disney family in 2019. Now National Geographic

ABOVE: Mickey Mouse
made his first theatrical
appearance in 1928
with the debut of
Walt's animated short
Steamboat Willie.

PAGES 10–11: Walt Disney
frequently used *National
Geographic* magazine to
find inspiration. Here he is
seen paging through his
collection to research
period costumes for a film.

is celebrating 100 Years of Wonder—the 100th anniversary of Disney's founding—along with The Walt Disney Company in 2023.

It's a natural partnership, as Walt was a scholar of a different kind: Although he never graduated high school, he was a lifelong learner, a voracious reader, and possessed an insatiable curiosity. He was an explorer, too; many of his best ideas came to him while he traveled the world. A futurist, he was fascinated with science and technology.

Walt valued research: "When we consider a new project, we really study it—not just the surface idea, but everything about it." *National Geographic* magazines were integral to this pursuit. An extensive library was installed at the studio during the 1930s; throughout the years, artists and designers

donated their personal copies. In the '90s, the entire collection was relocated to the Imagineering Resource Center, where it continues to serve as a source of inspiration.

An avid tourist, Walt brought back souvenirs, memories—and ideas! It was in New Orleans that Walt found a mechanical bird in a cage, which later inspired the lifelike creatures known as Audio-Animatronics figures. A road trip in Germany with his wife, Lilly, led to a serendipitous encounter with a monorail. Walt installed one later at Disneyland—the first one in North America.

Whatever the adventure, it doesn't have to be something grand and bucket list–worthy, or even risky; it can be as simple as discovering something hiding in plain sight, tasting a new treat, or trying an unexpected first-time experience: No matter what, it's all about excitement.

National Geographic believes "curiosity is for everyone." Walt had a like-minded philosophy: "When you're curious, you find lots of interesting things to do." With the spirit of curiosity—and adventure—in mind, this book curates 100 of the best Disney adventures across the globe. In the following pages, we've identified adventures in various categories, whether they're splurge-worthy travel experiences, fun for the whole family, recreational activities, or the simple joy of sharing a good meal. Some of the adventures are free. Others may remain on a wish list for a long time. But there is something for everyone.

As Ellie says in *Up*, "Adventure is out there!" ∎

THE HAPPIEST ADVENTURER ON EARTH

Walt knew that big ideas didn't happen sitting behind a desk. He was a globe-trotter because of both his wanderlust and his insatiable curiosity. "Always, as you travel," he reminds us, "assimilate the sounds and sights of the world." And assimilate he did! His adventures provided inspiration for dozens of our Disney favorites, from the books he collected in Europe that became classic films to architecture we recognize throughout Disneyland to the attractions that were influenced by treasures and trinkets he amassed on his travels—all because he was an adventurer, and, we think, the happiest adventurer of them all!

A: The astronomical clock in Strasbourg, France, was an inspiration for the "it's a small world" attraction's clock. B: Walt and his wife, Lilly, visited Mount Rainier, Washington. C: Walt enlisted in the Red Cross Ambulance Corps in 1918. He served in postwar France driving ambulances, making deliveries, and chauffeuring important officers. D: Walt visited Vancouver, British Columbia, many times; his last trip to the city was with his family in 1966.

A

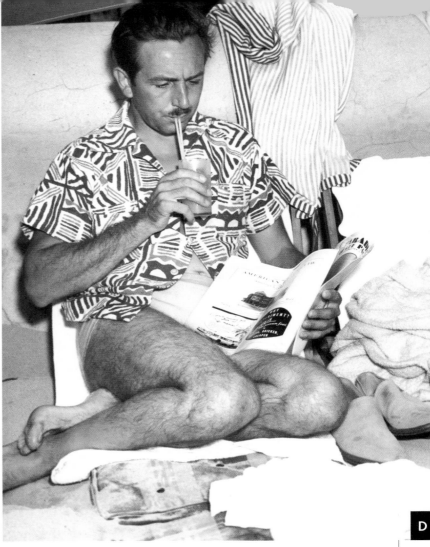

A: Walt took a trip to Alaska with his daughter Sharon in 1947. Alaska ended up being one of the filming locations for the Oscar-winning *Seal Island* (1948). B: On a trip to Germany, Walt saw an Alweg monorail, which ultimately inspired the Disneyland-Alweg Monorail System. C: In 1921, Walt founded the Laugh-O-gram Films studio. Though it ceased operation in 1923, many of Walt's pioneering efforts in animation began here. D: Walt's affection for Hawai'i, where he vacationed a number of times, inspired the Disney short *Hawaiian Holiday*, released in 1937.

A: Neuschwanstein Castle in Germany is famously one of the inspirations for Sleeping Beauty Castle at Disneyland. B: Walt visited Hawai'i a number of times, and the islands of Honolulu and Kaua'i (pictured here) served as filming locations for *Lt. Robin Crusoe, U.S.N.* (1966). C: Walt kept a vacation home in Smoke Tree Ranch, a hideaway tucked in the desert of Palm Springs, California. D: Tivoli Gardens in Denmark was one of Walt's favorite places and an inspiration for Disneyland. E: During a 1935 tour of Europe, Walt found loads of inspiration, including the Eiffel Tower and the Notre Dame Cathedral in Paris and the French Riviera.

CHAPTER ONE

LET'S GO FLY A KITE

Fun for All Ages

Watch one of Disney's iconic parades make its way down Main Street, U.S.A. in the Magic Kingdom at Walt Disney World.

TAKE A WALK DOWN MAIN STREET, U.S.A.

This Land Is Your Land

Main Street, U.S.A. was very important to Walt: It was partially inspired by his beloved hometown of Marceline, Missouri. "Many of us fondly remember our 'small hometown' and its friendly way of life at the turn of the century," Walt explained. "To me, this era represents an important part of our heritage, and thus we have endeavored to capture those years on Main Street, U.S.A. at Disneyland."

Main Street, U.S.A. in Disneyland runs from the railroad station, through Town Square (where Walt had an apartment above the Fire Department), to what Walt called the hub. He knew from studying amusement parks in Europe that people could easily get exhausted from walking and wanted a distinct central area convenient to all lands: "I planned it so each place is right off the hub . . . I don't want sore feet here. They make people tired and irritable. I want 'em to leave here happy. They'll be able to cover the whole place and not travel more than a couple of miles."

Walt also insisted that everything be authentic to the era, including an ice cream parlor, a marketplace where townsfolk would gather and gossip, eateries, a bakery, a movie theater, a penny arcade, and horse-drawn transportation. Tribute windows line the thoroughfare, celebrating the men and women who helped Walt build Disneyland, including one that honors Walt's father, Elias, above the Emporium.

MAIN STREET AT HOME

Bring a piece of the Disney parks to life in your own home! The Disney Parks Blog and Walt Disney Imagineering have partnered to design printable activity sheets for you to create 3D versions of your park favorites. All you need for the Disney Paper Parks kits are crayons, scissors, and glue.

OPPOSITE: The "Partners" statue was unveiled at Walt Disney World in 1995.

PAGES 22-3: Crystal Arts on Main Street, U.S.A. in Disneyland sells sparkling mementos that you can have engraved.

Imagineer and Disney Legend Marty Sklar was hired to write the 1890s-themed *Disneyland News*. Marty was hard-pressed to understand how Walt had the time to "worry about . . . a ten-cent newspaper to be sold on Main Street." However, soon Marty realized why. "It was a story and a detail. That's what Disneyland is about, stories and details." For Walt, Main Street, U.S.A. was a real place. Every small town in America had a paper, and Walt's town would have one, too.

Notably, Main Street, U.S.A. began at Disneyland, and it is the only one of the parks' main streets that Walt ever walked on. Since then, every Disney resort has included a main street, continuing Walt's wish that guests are greeted by a welcoming and cheerful land.

Main Street, U.S.A. in the Magic Kingdom at Walt Disney World is inspired by an amalgam of many towns, including Saratoga, New York—and its Norman Rockwell feel—as teased in the promotional brochure. It shares similar features to those at Disneyland, including Town Square, City Hall, and the Emporium; however, it's much bigger and has unique businesses and restaurants.

WALK THIS WAY

Walt spent weeks working on Disneyland's curbing. "Well, it's very important that Main Street isn't too big, and it can't be too small," he said. "Because if it's too wide and nobody's in the park and people come in and they'll think there's nobody there. On the other hand, if it's not wide enough, when there's a crowd there, it'll be too congested." Walt delighted that he could "jaywalk" on his Main Street, U.S.A.

OPPOSITE: The Emporium on Main Street, U.S.A. lights up as day turns to night in Hong Kong Disneyland.

ABOVE: Every Main Street, U.S.A. at a Disney theme park is designed to resemble a small American town at the turn of the 20th century.

Tokyo Disneyland has World Bazaar, which showcases its main street running through the center of the land. Because of the city's inclement weather, it is covered entirely by a roof.

Main Street, U.S.A. at Disneyland Paris gives guests in France an opportunity to experience the good old-fashioned U.S.A. Liberty Arcade tells the story of the Statue of Liberty, while Discovery Arcade displays 19th-century inventions.

Shanghai Disneyland is the only park where the main thoroughfare is not called Main Street. Instead, guests enter from Mickey Avenue. This is a fitting tribute to the "mouse that started it all" and the character Walt credits with creating his empire. International in spirit, Mickey Avenue reflects a sense of geography with Chinese influences as well.

Whichever main street you stroll in the world, Walt welcomes you. ∎

FAMILY FUN ON THE FRONTIER

The Hoop-Dee-Doo Musical Revue at Fort Wilderness Resort & Campground

The Hoop-Dee-Doo Musical Revue opened on September 5, 1974. Although Walt passed away eight years before the first performance, the much beloved revue at Disney's Fort Wilderness Resort & Campground is a live stage show created in the vein of both the Diamond Horseshoe Revue at the Magic Kingdom and its predecessor, the Golden Horseshoe Revue at Disneyland (one of Walt's favorite attractions in his original Magic Kingdom). Claire de Lune, Johnny Ringo, Dolly Drew, Six Bits Slocum, Flora Long, and Jim Handy star in the audience participation production at Pioneer Hall. Stomp your feet and clap your hands during a sing-along or two. A few guests are invited—sometimes coaxed—onstage and are cast as characters in the frontier saga, so if you're the shy type, prepare to squirm in good fun. The show is accompanied by an all-you-can-eat family-style meal that includes the restaurant's signature dish, fried chicken (also a favorite of Walt's).

For many Disney families, returning to Fort Wilderness Resort & Campground is an annual tradition. It's close to the Magic Kingdom yet feels entirely remote with its unique camping opportunity. Staying at the RV campsites and furnished cabins is always a rootin' tootin' time. Recreation offerings include archery lessons and guided fishing excursions. Motorized boats, canoes, and kayaks are available for rental on Bay Lake. There are also pools with waterslides, basketball courts, playgrounds, and beach volleyball.

HORSING AROUND

Western shows go way back with Disney. In 1955, Walt personally hired gagman and Disney Legend Wally Boag to star in the Golden Horseshoe Revue. He performed the show so many times that he was put in the *Guinness Book of World Records*. In 1971, Wally opened the same show in the Magic Kingdom at The Diamond Horseshoe.

OPPOSITE: Sing, dance, and have a wild good time at the Hoop-Dee-Doo Musical Revue in Pioneer Hall.

PAGES 28-9: Disney's Fort Wilderness Resort & Campground has roughly 800 campsites, fit for everything from tents to RVs.

For a different way to explore the 750-acre (300-ha) pine and cypress forest, try the Wilderness Back Trail Adventure. On the beautiful and easy walking trails through the Florida countryside, you'll find plenty of photo stops, including the always becoming Bay Lake.

Want s'more old-fashioned family fun? Take part in Chip 'n' Dale's Campfire Sing-A-Long. Roast marshmallows with your hosts, Disney's favorite larger-than-life chipmunks. If you get the two confused, Chip has the black nose, just like a chocolate chip. Be sure to stay for the complimentary movies in the Meadow. Set in the outdoor amphitheater, it's one of the most enticing venues in all of Walt Disney World for the Disney Movie Under the Stars program.

A resort themed to the American frontier would not be complete without horses. There are trail, pony, and wagon rides, even a "sleigh" during the holidays in December. Explore Tri-Circle-D Ranch and see the ponies that pull Cinderella's carriage and the equine cast members of Main Street, U.S.A. Don't miss the working blacksmith shop.

FUN FACT

Fort Wilderness Resort & Campground has a unique distinction in all of Walt Disney World. In the thousands of acres purchased for the vacation capital of the world, Walt and Roy only walked the property that was later developed as Fort Wilderness.

OPPOSITE: Fried chicken is on the menu during the Hoop-Dee-Doo Musical Revue.

ABOVE: Fort Wilderness Resort offers tons of ways to get outside, from canoeing and kayaking to horseback riding and FootGolf.

After the sun sets, wrangle your crew and head to the Fort Wilderness beach and marina to watch the magical illuminated sea creatures of the Electrical Water Pageant.

A big part of the Fort Wilderness culture is the golf carts. Whether you bring your own or rent one on-site, everyone is encouraged to use their imaginations and customize their ride—especially for the parades. As opposed to those in the parks, these parades feature guests as the stars. Every Fourth of July, Halloween, and Christmas there is a cavalcade of carts that winds its way through the resort. If you're not participating, stake a claim along the route and enjoy the spectacle.

And if all this doesn't keep the family busy, the Magic Kingdom is just a boat ride away. ∎

TO INFINITY AND BEYOND!

Join Woody and Buzz at the Toy Story Hotel

"If you sit on a shelf for the rest of your life, you'll never find out." —Woody
Heed Woody's advice and head to Shanghai Disneyland! For anyone who's longed to play with the gang of Disney/Pixar's *Toy Story* films, this resort is for you. The hotel's entrance resembles oversize packaging (and the debate over whether you leave collectibles in their box or play with them may commence). Once in the lobby, you're immersed in a land of fun and frolic celebrating the four-film blockbuster franchise. Signs are not printed; they are left for Etch A Sketch. Columns are constructed with what else? Building blocks. Here, the toys come "alive," even when grown-ups are around.

The rooms are reminiscent of all things *Toy Story* with Sheriff Woody carpet, Rubik's Cube nightstands, and, of course, the clouds of Andy's room.

The Launch Pad is an interactive water play area featuring the *Toy Story* aliens. With the Claw—their master—nowhere to be found, they prepare to take off in the rocket; water mist sprays from all angles as they attempt to launch. If you needed another reason to select this resort, this experience is exclusive to hotel guests.

Or consider Tokyo Disney Resort, where guests will feel like they've been shrunk to the size of a toy. The lobby sports a jigsaw puzzle–inspired floor, and the ceiling is designed to look like a board game.

Whether you are a Cowboy, Space Ranger, Potato Head, or mere mortal, you'll have a friend at the Toy Story Hotel. ∎

You might spot characters like Woody and Jessie around the Toy Story Hotel.

HOWLIDAY HAPPENINGS

Celebrate Halloween the Disney Way

Whether you like to be scared out of your wits or prefer watching others get tricked, Halloween with Disney is guaranteed to be spooktacular!

Disney and Halloween go all the way back to *The Skeleton Dance*, the whimsically macabre cartoon that debuted in 1929. Decades later, family-friendly Halloween parties premiered at Disneyland and the Magic Kingdom. Now, Oogie Boogie Bash—A Disney Halloween Party at Disney California Adventure Park and Mickey's Not-So-Scary Halloween Party in the Magic Kingdom at Walt Disney World are specially ticketed events that happen in the evening after the parks close: Attend wearing your costume (not allowed during normal park operating hours for those 14 and older), become bewitched by not-too-creepy cavalcades, and trick-or-treat, of course!

The first major attraction to receive a Halloween overlay (a term for temporary retheming) was the Haunted Mansion at Disneyland. Based on *Tim Burton's The Nightmare Before Christmas* (1993), the "Master of Scare-omonies" Jack Skellington redecorates the spook house, combining Halloween Town and Christmas. The Haunted Mansion Holiday experience runs seasonally. It's also available at Tokyo Disneyland, where parades have featured a skeleton-operated float themed to the park's railroad, with Mickey as the engineer.

"MahaloWeen" is celebrated at Trader Sam's bars in both Disneyland and

WICKED FUN

What would Halloween be without villains? At Hong Kong Disneyland, the Wicked Fun Party Zone is an opportunity to meet them up close. This is Disney, so there will be an upbeat celebration, too: Mickey's Halloween Street Party, with Mickey leading the parade atop a giant jack-o'-lantern.

OPPOSITE: Hades is projected onto Cinderella Castle at Walt Disney World.

PAGES 36-7: Travel through the looking glass with the Mad Hatter at Oogie Boogie Bash—A Disney Halloween Party in Disneyland.

Walt Disney World. Tropical drinks are served in limited-edition Halloween tiki mugs, and special effects abound. The very first mug was based on Disney Legend Blaine Gibson's original sculpture of the Haunted Mansion's Hatbox Ghost. The illusion, where the ghost's head disappears from his shoulders and reappears in the box he holds in his hand, was created by Disney Legend Yale Gracey.

Get in the spooky spirit at Disney parks around the world. Disney's Halloween Festival is wicked fun at Disneyland Paris and features Captain Hook, Cruella, Maleficent, and other villains.

Mickey's Halloween Street Party and the musical stage show "Let's Get Wicked" are highlights of the celebrations at Hong Kong Disneyland.

Cosplay is very popular in Japan. That makes Halloween a favorite time of year for guests to dress in costumes—sometimes elaborately—at Tokyo Disneyland and Tokyo DisneySea.

If you are staying home to pass out candy to the little ghosts and goblins, you might want to watch *Trick or Treat* (1952) starring Donald Duck on Disney+. ∎

A SPIRITED CRUISE

From late September to November, commemorate Halloween on the High Seas on a Disney cruise. Pack your costumes for Mickey's Mousequerade. Participate in *Tim Burton's The Nightmare Before Christmas* (1993) Sing and Scream interactive movie experience. And learn about Día de Los Muertos—including lessons about our departed ancestors in *Coco* (2017)—on a Cozumel excursion.

A HAPPY HALLOWEEN

There is magical mischief in all the Disney parks, but what if you can't be there in person? How about watching a Disney movie to get you in the spirit: *The Adventures of Ichabod and Mr. Toad* (1949); *Escape to Witch Mountain* (1975); *The Black Cauldron* (1985); *Tim Burton's The Nightmare Before Christmas* (1993); *Hocus Pocus* (1993); *Monsters, Inc.* (2001); *Maleficent* (2014); or *Muppets Haunted Mansion* (2021). You can also carve pumpkins using templates downloaded from *disneyparks.disney.go.com,* with designs varying in difficulty from an easy Skeleton Mickey to a moderate Princess Anna or a complex Dr. Facilier. And for foolish mortals, learn how to make a Haunted Mansion Butler Halloween costume on the Disney Parks YouTube channel.

A: Celebrate the season with the Haunted Mansion Gravediggers during Mickey's "Boo-to-You" Halloween Parade. B: Mickey and Minnie get into the Halloween spirit at Mickey's Not-So-Scary Halloween Party in the Magic Kingdom. C: The Headless Horseman leads Mickey's "Boo-to-You" Halloween Parade at the Magic Kingdom. D: The parks get a makeover during Halloween, with surprises like Pumpkin Mickey in Disneyland at every corner. E: Don't forget to try the special Halloween version of the Mickey Waffle sundae at the Magic Kingdom. F: In Plaza de la Familia at Disneyland, the world of *Coco* (2017) comes to life with the spirit of Día de los Muertos. G: Costumed Chip and Dale take part in the fun at Mickey's Not-So-Scary Halloween Party. H: A trick and a treat? Worms and Dirt from the Magic Kingdom is a frightfully delicious snack.

A

B

C

E

F

G

H

MEET THE OTHER BEAST

Disney castles traditionally don't have dungeons—with the exception of Disneyland Paris. At the base of Le Château de la Belle au Bois Dormant (French for Sleeping Beauty Castle), the sign "La Tanière du Dragon" tempts.

Entering the dark walk-through attraction, venture along the stalactites in the cavernlike lair until you reach the pool of water and the beast. The dragon is chained and appears to be dreaming, his talons and tail moving ever so slightly. When he awakens—slightly startled and possibly grumpy—he raises his head and breathes fire, with just the right amount of intensity for small children.

Considering the location, it's easy to assume the beast is Maleficent; however, he belongs to Merlin, who also resides in the castle. The attraction's backstory shares a thread with *The Fox and the Hound* (1981), where Merlin and the dragon have been friends since childhood. The dragon is not a captive nor is the shackle a punishment; consider it more of a pet leash.

At the time Walt Disney Imagineering constructed the dragon for the 1992 debut, it was one of the largest Audio-Animatronics figures in the world. It remains one of the most impressive.

Before you bid adieu, visit the sorcerer's cave nearby. Known as Merlin l'Enchanteur, this medieval shop is where you'll find magical and fantastical souvenirs.

STARK (VIRTUAL) REALITY

A Superhero-Worthy Experience With Iron Man

When Marvel joined the Disney family, Iron Man became the first superhero in the series to star in a Disney theme park attraction: the Iron Man Experience. Tomorrowland is about the future, and that's fittingly where you will find the 3D thriller at Hong Kong Disneyland.

The action-packed premise has Iron Man's alter ego, Tony Stark, choosing Hong Kong (a center of world technology) to host Stark Expo. His company is known for changing the world for the better, thus he's displaying his latest high-tech inventions and innovations. The Expo's halls also serve as the ride's queue: The gravity-defying Iron Wing is found in the Hall of Mobility; the Hall of Protection features an up close look at the Iron Man Mark III suit; and the arc reactor, which produces enough energy to sustain an entire city, is located in the Hall of Energy.

Once through the halls, guests receive 3D StarkVision glasses before boarding the Expo Edition Iron Wing flight vehicle, complete with artificial intelligence, armor plating, and self-healing glass. With Iron Man by your side, you'll soar over Hong Kong, past mountains, above Victoria Harbour, under bridges, and along the streets as you battle the evil forces of Hydra.

The Iron Man Tech Showcase features the Become Iron Man game—your chance to emulate the genius inventor and Avenger. ∎

Step into the world of Stark Industries for a heroic 3D experience.

THAT'S SEW MICKEY

Customize Your Mouse Ears With Park Embroidery

"Eighty-five years and still wearing Ears." —As seen on a guest's shirt in the Magic Kingdom

There are ears (hats and headbands) for every occasion: birthdays, weddings, anniversaries, special events, attractions, Disney movies and characters; ears that resemble cast member costumes, such as train conductor caps and The Twilight Zone Tower of Terror bellhop hats; interactive ears that are synchronized with parades and shows; even ones created by top fashion designers including Vera Wang, Loungefly, and COACH. Ears are sold throughout the park in several shops, some with exclusive and unique offerings. Disney ears also include designs inspired by Pixar, Marvel, and *Star Wars*—everything from panda-inspired looks from *Turning Red* (2022) to R2D2 and even Captain America.

Snack-inspired ears showcasing park favorites such as popcorn and pretzels are always popular. And some are ear-resistible, such as a beignet headband scented with the delicious aroma of the puffy powdered doughnut.

The tradition of having ears with custom embroidery began when Disneyland opened in 1955. In those days, a cast member would guide the hat on a special sewing machine, spelling the name in script; now an automated machine does the job.

You will find hundreds of options for ears at the parks, in the resorts, and on shopDisney.

Disney ear etiquette dictates taking them off and stowing them for fast rides so they don't fly off. Nothing says "I love Disney!" more than iconic Disney ears! ∎

Make it personal with Mickey ears embroidered at the parks.

EARS THROUGH THE YEARS

Three simple circles have emerged as the iconic headwear for many Disney fans, but where did they get their start? That takes us all the way back to 1929 and the black-and-white animated short *The Karnival Kid*, where Mickey Mouse tips his "ears" to Minnie. Later, in 1955, when the *Mickey Mouse Club* debuted on television, staff artist and Disney Legend Roy Williams used that tip of the ears as inspiration to create hats for the young cast. Since then, Disney ears have evolved. However, the basic Mickey ears that started it all remain incredibly popular.

A: While Mickey dons a sailor's cap, you can wear your own sparkly ears aboard the *Disney Dream* cruise ship. B: Special-edition ears pay homage to various Disney attractions and films, like the Band Director Mickey ear headband (left) and Minnie ears with special bows (right). C: Baseball hats have gotten the Mickey and Minnie treatment, too. D: These ears even paid homage to Mickey's bottom, with a fun nod to his iconic red pants, buttons, and tail. E: In 1977, a syndicated version of the *Mickey Mouse Club* ran—in color—with a new cast of 12 and new Mickey ears. F: Embroidery isn't just for us—it's for the big mouse on campus, too. "Happy Birthday, Mickey" ears were spotted at Comic-Con in 2018. G: Totally original: The first mouse ear hats were created for the cast of the *Mickey Mouse Club* variety show in the 1950s. H: Magical Mickey moments are just a part of the joy of visiting a Disney park.

A

D

B

C

E

F

WALT DISNEY
6929
S303 "THE MICKEY MOUSE CLUB"
RECTOR

G

H

CELEBRATE AMERICA

Attend an Iconic Flag Retreat

Walt's daughter Diane Disney Miller reminisced: "He'd watch the flag lowering at Disneyland every evening they were down there and tears would flow down his cheeks."

This may be one of the most overlooked moments at the park—and another way to stay connected to the traditions that were near and dear to Walt. He was a proud American and patriot, saying, "Actually, if you could see close in my eyes, the American flag is waving in both of them and up my spine is growing this red, white, and blue stripe." So it wasn't surprising that he instituted the flag retreat—a ritual dating back to his hero Abraham Lincoln's presidency—on Opening Day of Disneyland on July 17, 1955.

To this day, every afternoon in Town Square, the Disneyland Security Honor Guard lowers the flag and retires the colors. Often, they are accompanied by the Disneyland Band and, on special occasions such as Veterans Day, by the Dapper Dans (Disneyland's beloved barbershop quartet in stripes). The anthems for the Army, Marine Corps, Navy, Air Force, and Coast Guard are played as military personnel are invited to encircle the flagpole when their branch of service is called. Everyone is encouraged to sing along to "The Star-Spangled Banner" and other patriotic melodies.

The Magic Kingdom at Walt Disney World also has a flag retreat and its own unique tradition: selecting a veteran or active duty service member at random and inviting them to participate in the ceremony, which includes the honor of marching down Main Street, U.S.A. holding the folded American flag.

Bring your children and be prepared to shed a tear or two. ∎

Mickey thanks retired Tuskegee Airmen, guests of honor at the ritual flag retreat, held daily in Disneyland since Walt founded the park.

SUIT UP

Superheroes Unite Throughout the Avengers Campus

Heroes assemble! Avengers Campus is the newest addition to Disney California Adventure Park, opened in 2021. And there are plenty of ways to get in on the action: Decode the mysteries of the multiverse with Doctor Strange in the Ancient Sanctum. Ride along as Rocket rescues his friends from the Collector's Fortress on Guardians of the Galaxy—Mission: BREAKOUT! On WEB SLINGERS: A Spider-Man Adventure, Peter Parker's Spider-Bots are replicating out of control and Spidey needs help to trap them all.

Hungry? Foe fighters get famished, too. There are two epic eateries on campus: The Shawarma Palace pays homage to Tony Stark's last lines in *Marvel's The Avengers* (2012)—"Have you ever tried shawarma? There's a shawarma joint about two blocks from here. I don't know what it is, but I want to try it." Now you can try the Middle Eastern classic, too. The Pym Test Kitchen uses Ant-Man and the Wasp's "Pym Particles" technology to shrink and grow the fare, from tiny treats to massive mains. The restaurant is situated in an old lab where remnants of past experiments are on display. This is the perfect place to power up.

It wouldn't be the home of superheroes without stunts. And who better to showcase the versatility of Earth's Mightiest Heroes than Spider-Man? He puts on a daily demonstration that includes tumbling, web crawling, scaling buildings, and the mightiest leap across a building you'll ever see up close. Be on the lookout for other superheroes from across time and space, including Black Panther, Captain Marvel, Black Widow, Ant-Man, the Wasp, and Thor— always on the ready to defend Avengers Headquarters. Will you be the next recruit? ∎

Enter a towering citadel on Guardians of the Galaxy— Mission: BREAKOUT! to help rescue Star-Lord, Gamora, Drax, and Groot.

A MAGICAL MILESTONE

Get Your Child's First Haircut on Main Street, U.S.A.

Whether you've been counting the days or have finally mustered the courage to trim the locks they were born with, consider Harmony Barber Shop in Walt Disney World for your child's first haircut.

Nestled in Town Square near the fire station, the requisite red-white-and-blue barber's pole stands out front. The shop's Main Street, U.S.A. setting is authentic to a typical 1900s-era barbershop in small-town America. It may appear as another fictitious business, but it is in fact a real, working establishment staffed by state-licensed barbers and cosmetologists. The cast members have a lot of experience with children, playfully informing them every step of the way to put them at ease. And because this is Walt Disney World, glitter, sparkles, and pixie dust abound, too. Occasionally the Magic Kingdom barbershop quartet—the Dapper Dans—arrives to delight the parents.

The milestone celebration includes an official "First Haircut" certificate, a keepsake of the shorn tresses, and commemorative "My First Haircut" Mickey Mouse ears. Peter Pan warned us to never grow up, however, so adults are welcome, too.

This is a very popular experience on Main Street, U.S.A. in the Magic Kingdom, the only Disney park in the world to have a barbershop. Reservations are taken as far as 180 days in advance, and they fill quickly. ∎

A haircut at Harmony Barber Shop has been a beloved park experience since the Magic Kingdom opened in 1971.

MEET DUFFY

Mickey's Plush Companion Has Captivated Millions of Fans

Before Duffy became Duffy, he was called *The Disney Bear* at Walt Disney World. He was then introduced to Tokyo DisneySea with a brand-new story by Imagineers and came to life as Duffy. The rest is history: He became the most popular teddy bear ever in Japan, with enthusiastic fans dressing him, taking him everywhere, and even dining with him. Why such a craze? The story of Minnie making a stuffed bear to keep sea captain Mickey company on his lonely voyages resonated with the Japanese sensibility of caring for one another, and, of course, Duffy definitely struck the Japanese "kawaii culture" chord. Let's face it: He is cute and fluffy and has the most innocent and caring personality. It's hard not to smile when you hold him.

Responding to overwhelming demand, Imagineers have created six additional friends over 12 years, each with a distinct personality: ShellieMay (a caring and crafty bear); Gelatoni (an artist cat with an eye to see beauty in everything); StellaLou (a spunky rabbit determined to become a Broadway dancer); CookieAnn (an inventive dog who loves to cook); 'Olu Mel (a kind-hearted ukulele-playing turtle in touch with nature); and LinaBell (an inquisitive, intelligent, detective-like fox). They are exclusive merchandise in the Disney parks in Asia and at Aulani, A Disney Resort & Spa in Hawai'i. Like Duffy, they all come to life in Mickey's and our imaginations. Fans wait for hours and hours just to get their favorite friends, costumes, and accessories. Duffy and Friends have become a *lifestyle*—fans live and breathe them, and their photos are ubiquitous on social media. At the end of the day, we all need a friend who makes us smile. ∎

Duffy's design pays homage to his dear friend Mickey—pay close attention to the markings on his face.

TAKE A TRIP TO TUNDRATOWN

The first *Zootopia*-themed land is coming soon. Fans of Judy Hopps, Nick Wilde, and Flash—the Department of Mammal Vehicles (DMV) worker in super-duper slow motion—will travel to Shanghai Disneyland to experience the mammal metropolis. The park will be Shanghai Disneyland's eighth themed land. The attractions will seamlessly blend Disney storytelling and state-of-the-art technology, and food and entertainment complete the package. The guests are fellow Zootopia citizens in this fully immersive land based on the 2017 Academy Award–winning animated movie.

THE WALT DISNEY FAMILY MUSEUM

"My goals were that our visitors would leave knowing my dad, inspired by his story, and that the whole experience would be a very pleasant one for them."

Those words were the inspiration for Walt's daughter Diane Disney Miller to co-found The Walt Disney Family Museum with her son Walter Elias Miller in San Francisco, California. The museum's mission is "to inform present and future generations about the man and, through his story, to inspire them to heed their imagination and persevere in pursuing their goals."

The entire experience is immersive and interactive—with plenty of hands-on exhibits. The scope of tremendous care given to each and every gallery is evident. The opportunity to hear stories from Walt himself, along with those who knew him, is truly magical.

It all starts the moment you enter the building. The Awards Lobby showcases some pretty spectacular artifacts, including Walt's honorary Oscar (featuring one standard-size and seven little statuettes) for *Snow White and the Seven Dwarfs* (1937) and a partial replica of his apartment at Disneyland, including Walt and Lillian's original furniture.

The first gallery is about Walt's childhood and teenage years, from his time in his hometown of Marceline, Missouri, to his Red Cross experience in France after World War I. Both shaped his future career. Learn how Walt sold Wolf River apples grown on the Disney family farm, delivered newspapers twice a day in Kansas City, and worked on the assembly line at his father's jelly factory in Chicago. Just a short walk away, and you are

OPPOSITE: The Walt Disney Family Museum is part of the Golden Gate National Recreation Area in San Francisco and celebrates the life and legacy of Walt.

PAGES 60-61: In the museum's main hall, see the Disneyland of Walt's imagination and the first versions of Audio-Animatronics figures.

introduced to Walt's first days working as an artist and filmmaker.

Next, you board an elevator cleverly designed to feel like a train car (a nod to Walt's journey to California), and the rest of Walt's life and career unfold. The subsequent galleries explore his move to Hollywood, the creation of Mickey Mouse, and the early development of the Walt Disney Studio. Exhibits demonstrate the transition from shorts to full-length films, his early production innovations, the expansion to live-action films, plus the *True-Life Adventures* (1948–1960) documentary series. The personal side of Walt has its own gallery, including part of his miniature collection, an intimate look at his home life, and precious family mementos. Disneyland fans will be enthralled with the custom model created for the museum that represents the Disneyland of Walt's imagination, including attractions of the past and those he envisioned but did not live to see. Peek inside Sleeping Beauty Castle for a sentimental touch: a miniature tribute to Walt and young Diane visiting the park together.

Walt passed away on December 15, 1966, just 10 days after turning 65. The last gallery is dedicated to his memory and features cards, tributes, and obituaries from around the world.

This being Disney, it ends on a happy note! The gift shop is packed with one-of-a-kind souvenirs, treasures, and trinkets.

The Walt Disney Family Museum is located at 104 Montgomery Street in the Presidio of San Francisco, California. ∎

WATCH THE NEON LIGHTS TURN ON AT DUSK IN CARS LAND

t's not advertised, not listed on daily schedules, and not to be missed.

Before leaving his new friends for the speedway and a chance at the Piston Cup, Lightning McQueen famously asked his pals in Cars (2006), "Is it getting dark out?" Then, with the help of Lizzie and Red, Radiator Springs' neon lights turn on for the first time in years. It's a magical moment that brings this stop on Route 66 back to life.

Cars Land at Disney California Adventure replicates that scene nightly just after sunset, complete with the accompanying song from the movie, "Sh-Boom." And seeing it in person is just as impressive as it is on-screen. As day turns to night, the street and lights turn on across the Carburetor County town, including Ramone's House of Body Art, Luigi's Casa Della Tires, Flo's V8 Café, the Cozy Cone Motel, and Sarge's Surplus Hut.

It's the ultimate way to shift into nighttime gear at the park.

LET YOUR PRINCESS SHINE

Get a Royal Makeover at Bibbidi Bobbidi Boutique

Cinderella isn't the only one who can have a fairy godmother grant a makeover.

That's because fairy tales do come true at Bibbidi Bobbidi Boutique. Here, cast members will transform your child (between three and 12 years old) into the Disney princess or knight of their dreams. This epic experience will make any birthday or celebration extra special.

At each Bibbidi Bobbidi Boutique around the world, your little one will be treated to a fantasy. Inside the one-of-a-kind storefront, they will feel like royalty the moment they enter the regal lobby. They'll be greeted by plush chairs, velvet drapes, majestic decorations, and, of course, gowns.

The gowns are more than just costumes; they are an enchanting part of the experience. Select from beloved characters, including Snow White, Tiana, Belle, Jasmine, Aurora, Rapunzel, Moana, Ariel, Tinker Bell, Merida, Mulan, Elsa, Anna, and Cinderella. Accessories include crowns, wands, fairy wings, spirit jerseys, and headbands. There are also costumes and accessories for those who want to be a gallant Disney knight.

And then there is the transformation—the kind that Disney is known for: the magical changes in appearance we see in many animated classics, such as when Ariel trades her mermaid tail for legs; when Pinocchio changes from a puppet to a boy; when Beast returns to his stately self; or when Tiana and Naveen transcend their frog forms and turn back to humans. This is the charm

THE MAGIC OF A SONG

"Bibbidi-Bobbidi-Boo" was written in 1948 by Mack David, Al Hoffman, and Jerry Livingston and sung by Verna Felton, who voiced the Fairy Godmother in the 1950 animated version of *Cinderella.* Also called "The Magic Song," the tune became a chart-topper covered by other artists, including Perry Como and Dinah Shore.

OPPOSITE: Dreams come true with magic from Disney's fairy godmothers.

PAGES 66-7: Princess gowns and knight costumes are displayed for guests to choose from.

of the Bibbidi Bobbidi adventure: Little ones walk into the boutique as a regular park guest and exit as their favorite character.

Parents have a front-row seat to the show, watching as the children—with their backs to a mirror that is covered by fabric—are primped and pampered in the salon. Then, with the wave of a magic wand—accompanied by pixie or dragon dust—the chair is turned for the big reveal. The curtain parts for the child's first look; the delight of the newly coronated is memory making at its finest.

For those at Walt Disney World—especially for children choosing Belle or Cinderella as their heroine—consider adding some extra magic to the occasion by making a reservation to dine at Be Our Guest Restaurant or Cinderella's Royal Table (page 262).

Reservations at Bibbidi Bobbidi Boutique are highly recommended and can be made up to 60 days in advance. Locations are at Disneyland Resort, Walt Disney World Resort, and Hong Kong Disneyland, and on Disney Cruise Line ships. ■

MORE FROM WALT

According to Disney Legend Marc Davis, Walt's favorite piece of animation in *Cinderella* (1950) was the transformation of Cinderella's dress. When Walt described the Fairy Godmother sequence, he said: "Have the miracle happen at the end of the song. 'The dream that you wish will come true' is where we start to bring the Fairy Godmother in. She materializes because she is there to grant the wish."

A LEGENDARY DESCENT

Have an Underwater Adventure Aboard Les Mystères du Nautilus

"With its untold depths, couldn't the sea keep alive such huge specimens of life from another age," wrote Jules Verne. "Couldn't the heart of the ocean hide the last-remaining varieties of these titanic species, for whom years are centuries and centuries millennia?"

The 20,000 Leagues Under the Sea attraction debuted at Disneyland in 1955; it's believed that Walt rolled up his sleeves and helped paint the giant squid the night before the park opened.

Based on the movie of the same name, which Walt produced, the actual sets from the 1954 film were installed to create the walk-through.

Now, Disneyland Paris has the distinction of being the only Disney park in the world to have an updated version of Walt's tribute to Captain Nemo. Just as the French author Jules Verne imagined it, this is a full-scale reproduction of Nemo's submarine.

The attraction in Discoveryland, which debuted in 1994, begins with a descent down the winding stairs, through an underwater tunnel, and into the 230-foot (70-m) sub. Traverse through the Ballasts Compartment, where the underwater adventurer's treasures are stored, and past the captain's cabin, resplendent with fine art, the crew quarters, chart room, and diving chamber. Next, the Grand Salon impresses with Nemo's organ. The last stop is the creaking engine room before returning to dry land. ∎

Walt Disney turned *20,000 Leagues Under the Sea* into a movie in 1954; today you can celebrate the literary and film classic in Disneyland Paris.

THE GREATEST SHOW ON EARTH

Attend One of Disney's Iconic Parades

Walt understood the power of emotion. It's evident in Disney movies, and it's evident in Disney parades, too. One of his heroes, Mark Twain, describes the visceral effect: "So far as I can see, a procession has value in but two ways—as a show and as a symbol, its minor function being to delight the eye, its major one to compel thought, exalt the spirit, stir the heart, and inflame the imagination."

Imagine sitting on the curb in anticipation, hearing the approaching music, catching a glimpse of the first float, singing along, while characters you've only seen in the movies wave to *you*, plus all the rapture that goes with a live and up close performance.

Disney and parades have a storied history that begins with Mickey Mouse's 1934 debut in the Macy's Santa Claus Parade (now known as the Macy's Thanksgiving Day Parade). Pluto, Horace Horsecollar, the Big Bad Wolf, and the Three Little Pigs balloons also debuted that same year.

When Disneyland opened in July 1955, there was a celebratory parade down Main Street, U.S.A. befitting the remarkable occasion. Family, friends, co-workers, celebrities, marching bands, floats, riders on horseback, antique cars, and a cavalcade of Disney characters joined Walt.

Later that year, on Thanksgiving, Disneyland showcased the very first holiday parade. Walt and Disney Legend Fess Parker, who portrayed Davy

500,000 TINY LIGHTS OF MAGIC

The Main Street Electrical Parade debuted at Disneyland in 1972. It was, as described in the theme song, a "spectacular festival pageant of nighttime magic and imagination in thousands of sparkling lights and electro-synth-magnetic musical sounds."

OPPOSITE: Mickey and Minnie wave to guests during the Disney Festival of Fantasy Parade in the Magic Kingdom.

PAGES 72-3: Chill out as you watch Anna, Elsa, Olaf, and Kristoff pass by in the Magic Happens Parade at Disneyland.

Crockett, led the festivities. Disney parks around the world continue the holiday tradition today.

Parade elements have evolved from simple to elaborate over the years—from the sheer size of the floats (some serving as rolling stages) to the larger-than-life characters, such as the fire-breathing Maleficent. Then there's the dazzling lighting and projection technology for the nighttime spectaculars. And the action: circus stunts on trampolines, confetti and bubble blasts—even snow! The parades are not limited to park streets; they appear on water, too, with floats that light up in neon colors and fireworks displays above the sails.

For many, it's a ritual to stake a spot and wait along the route until the parade begins. At Tokyo Disneyland, they take that a step further, using "leisure sheets"—compact, affordable, picnic-like blankets that guests can spread out at their preferred location. Culture dictates that no one moves them or steps on them.

Prime views may be available with dining packages. Wherever you watch, the wonder and whimsy are an adventure. ■

MORE FROM WALT

Walt once shared a story about not fearing failure and a boy who wanted to march in a parade: "The bandmaster needed a trombonist, so the boy signed up. He hadn't marched a block before the fearful noises from his horn caused two old ladies to faint and a horse to run away. The bandmaster demanded, 'Why didn't you tell me you couldn't play the trombone?' And the boy said, 'How did I know? I never tried before.'"

SHOWMANSHIP AT ITS FINEST

Although we often associate parades with the pavement in the parks, some take place on the water. Disney Kite-Tails at Animal Kingdom uses personal watercraft to pull larger-than-life kites high in the air. *The Lion King* (1994) is represented by kites inspired by Simba and Zazu; Baloo and King Louie represent *The Jungle Book* (1967). The Electrical Water Pageant takes place in the Seven Seas Lagoon of Walt Disney World. The floating parade features sea creatures and a patriotic procession. At Disneyland, the Rivers of America is the stage for Fantasmic! With Mickey as host, it showcases more than 50 live performers, massive sets, stunning effects, and dazzling pyrotechnics.

A: Mickey is the star of the show, dressed appropriately as a wizard, at the Magic Happens Parade in Disneyland. B: Rapunzel and Flynn Rider make waves during Fantasmic! at Disneyland. C: Peter Pan and Wendy cruise by—with the help of a little pixie dust—during the Disney Festival of Fantasy Parade. D: Clarabelle Cow and friends spread the holiday cheer during Mickey's Very Merry Christmas Party in the Magic Kingdom. E: Boats and floats light up the Seven Seas Lagoon during the Electrical Water Pageant. F: Ulf the mime comes untangled in the Magic Kingdom. G: Disney KiteTails sends characters from *The Lion King* (1994) soaring over the waters in Disney's Animal Kingdom. H: A dream come true: Disney Dreamers Academy members joined a parade at the Magic Kingdom.

A

D

B

C

E

F

G

H

BE A DISNEY INSIDER

D23 Expo and a Tour of The Walt Disney Studios

C ome one, come all to the superfan experience of a lifetime. D23 is Disney's official fan club. *D* stands for Disney and *23* represents 1923, the year Walt arrived in Los Angeles and, with his brother Roy, founded what would become The Walt Disney Company. Established in 2009, D23 is the first ever club of its kind in the history of The Walt Disney Company. If you love Disney, want insider access, and enjoy spending time with others who share the same passion—this is for you! General Membership is complimentary. Upgrade to a Gold Member-ship for extra perks and special gifts, including a subscription to D23's exclusive *Disney twenty-three* publication, limited-edition theme park and movie-themed collectibles, and invitations to special events and screenings.

Here's a sampling of the one-of-a-kind experiences that await: D23 Expo is the biggest Disney fan event in the world and the ultimate "E ticket." Held under one roof at the Anaheim Convention Center, all the wonderful worlds of Disney are celebrated, including the best of Marvel, Pixar, *Star Wars,* television, streaming, and theme parks, with products, music, and entertainment. Cosplay is encouraged and those who partici-pate can compete in the Mousequerade costume contest for fun prizes and bragging rights. One can spend hours roaming the show floor point-ing, people-watching, and taking photos with the "characters." Collectors can find exclusive merchandise. Several stages showcase panels and presentations featuring favorite actors, Broadway performers, film direc-tors, Imagineers, and Disney creators of all kinds. Be the first to see trailers

OPPOSITE: The ultimate fan club, D23 puts on a biannual Expo where the latest and greatest in Disney films, television shows, streaming, books, and characters are shared and revealed.

PAGES 78-9: The Seven Dwarfs overlook Disney Legends Plaza—six are 19 feet (5.8 m) tall, but Dopey, holding up the cen-ter of the building, stands at only 12 feet (3.7 m).

for upcoming live-action and animated features; as a bonus, the stars often make appearances. Oh, and you'll see exclusive Disney parks previews, too!

Speaking of exclusive, how about getting inside the studio gates? Walt was just 38 years old when The Walt Disney Studios in Burbank, California, began operating in 1940. He and his brother Roy had outgrown their previous studio on Hyperion Avenue, the site where Mickey Mouse was born and where the first ever full-length animated feature, *Snow White and the Seven Dwarfs* (1937), was made. These successes paid for the state-of-the-art facility that is still home to Disney animation today.

The Walt Disney Studios is a closed campus; however, fans have an opportunity to experience it. D23 offers tours for Gold Members, and it's easy to see why they sell out so quickly. The day includes a visit to the original Animation Building, where classics such as *Cinderella* (1950), *Lady and the Tramp* (1955), and *The Jungle Book* (1967)—the last animated film Walt supervised—were created.

EXPO! EXPO! READ ALL ABOUT IT!

Pro tips for attending D23 Expo: Stay close to the Anaheim Convention Center; there's already a lot of walking on the Expo's floors. Talk to strangers, even though there really aren't strangers in Disney culture; everyone has a tip (or 23) they'd like to share. Pack water and snacks—you could find yourself waiting in line for coveted presentations. Bring a marker, and be prepared when asking for an autograph. Oh, and have fun!

OPPOSITE: D23 Expo is the chance to see sneak peeks of film announcements, like *Onward* (2020), announced at the 2017 Expo.

ABOVE: The Expo is a true celebration of all things Disney and includes special live performances and celebrity appearances.

Fans of live-action Disney films will enjoy seeing the soundstages where *20,000 Leagues Under the Sea* (1954) and *Mary Poppins* (1964) were made, along with many other fan-favorite films.

The grounds are a treat! You'll likely recognize the exterior spaces that have been used in many productions, including *Saving Mr. Banks* (2013), and the trademark water tower. Explore Disney Legends Plaza and the bronze handprints of Disney Legends, the highest honor awarded to those who have contributed to the Disney legacy.

Still, the best is yet to come! Visit the Walt Disney Archives, home of several of the company's historical collections. The pièce de résistance is an experience that any fan of Walt Disney will treasure: a tour of his office, Suite 3H, which has been faithfully restored to be accurate to the day he last used it in 1966. ∎

JUST AROUND THE RIVER BEND

Go Wild Aboard a Jungle River Cruise

Based on Disney's *True-Life Adventures* films (1948–1960), the Jungle Cruise was an Opening Day attraction at California's Disneyland in 1955. Decades later, the eponymous attraction inspired a movie by the same name in 2021.

Walt was involved with every detail of this epic adventure, which may have been partially inspired by a trip to South America in 1941. Initially, Walt wanted to have real animals; however, practicality prevailed. When it came to fabricating the critters, he was known to act out their movements for his Imagineers to replicate, even suggesting how an elephant's trunk should move.

The attraction has evolved and transformed, also appearing at the Magic Kingdom at Walt Disney World and Tokyo Disneyland. But the king of the jungle, many believe, is located at Hong Kong Disneyland. Guests choose the language spoken by their skipper: Cantonese, Putonghua, or English. The eight-minute cruise on the Rivers of Adventure features some of the classic gags from the American parks, as well as some unique to Hong Kong.

However, the finale of the Hong Kong park's attraction sets it apart from the others: the showstopping eruption in the legendary Canyon of the Gods. Dodge exploding springs, be dazzled by pyrotechnics and colorful lighting, and observe the wrath of the fire-breathing deity before returning safely to the dock.

Don't be in de-Nile: Ride the Jungle Cruise at Hong Kong Disneyland. ∎

Spot hippos and other wildlife aboard the Jungle River Cruise in Hong Kong Disneyland.

MARCELINE AND THE WALT DISNEY HOMETOWN MUSEUM

Although Walt only lived in Marceline, Missouri, for four years, its impact on him lasted a lifetime. "I hope the youth of today and the future know a childhood as happy as was mine in Marceline," he remarked. Walt talked about Marceline so often and with such affection that it wasn't until after his daughters were grown that they realized he was not born and raised there.

Kansas Avenue is considered one of the influences for Main Street, U.S.A. Walt was inspired by several structures along Marceline's thoroughfare when designing Disneyland. The Zurcher Building is strikingly similar to the Refreshment Corner, hosted by Coca-Cola. The Uptown Theater resembles the Main Street Cinema. Be sure to read the name tag of the ticket taker—a tribute to Tilly from Marceline.

Walt credits the birth of his imagination to the days he spent drawing under his "Dreaming Tree" on the Disney family farm, a bucolic plot his father purchased from a Civil War veteran's estate in 1906. The farm's barn is also where Walt put on his first show—a "circus" of stars including a goat, a pig, and a dog in costumes. Walt re-created this childhood barn in his Los Angeles backyard amid his personal railroad (see page 128). The original barn did not survive past the 1930s; however, it was rebuilt in 2001. There is no fee to visit Walt's Barn; it's open from sunrise to sunset. Bring a pen and leave a message

OPPOSITE: The Walt Disney Hometown Museum celebrates the place Walt called home—and the largest inspiration for Main Street, U.S.A.

PAGES 86-7: All aboard! Walt (left), then California governor Goodwin Knight (center), and Fred Gurley (right), president of the Santa Fe Railway, ride the *E. P. Ripley* to survey Disneyland.

on the interior walls, a tradition enjoyed by guests from around the world.

Wanting the Disney family story to be told in Marceline, Walt's little sister, Ruth, entrusted life-long Marceline resident Kaye Malins with her personal collection of memorabilia. Working alongside her parents, Inez and Rush, Kaye established the Walt Disney Hometown Museum, which opened on the occasion of what would have been Walt's 100th birthday.

The galleries, story stations, and railroad exhibit tell the history of one of the world's greatest story-tellers and innovators. Highlights include personal letters written between Disney family members from the early 1900s to the late 1960s, a miniature of Disneyland by Dale Varner (using blueprints that Walt personally sent to him), plus a riveting record-ing Walt made on his parents' 50th anniversary—there are only three copies in the world!

Visit these other complimentary Disney attrac-tions to complete your pilgrimage to Marceline: E.P. Ripley Park, where Walt played as a child (he later named the first steam engine at Disneyland the *E.P. Ripley*); Walt Disney Post Office (the only federal building named for Walt Disney); Walt Disney Elementary School, home to a custom mural commissioned by Walt; a flagpole from the 1960 Squaw Valley Olympics (Walt helped pro-duce the pageantry); and the retired Disneyland ride Midget Autopia, currently being restored, a gift from Walt and Roy in 1966.

The Walt Disney Hometown Museum is located at 120 E Santa Fe Avenue in Marceline, Missouri. ∎

GIZMOS AND GADGETS

The Disney Parks apps help you plan and enhance your visit. But there is more fun to be had on your smartphone at Disneyland and Walt Disney World: Play Disney Parks. Waiting in line has never gone by more quickly or with more glee. Enjoy activities that interact with attraction queues and games that immerse you in the stories of Disney, earning digital collectibles for your achievements along the way.

Adventures abound in *Star Wars: Galaxy's Edge*—hack into droids, scan crates, tune into transmissions, translate languages, and find plenty more to discover as you create your own *Star Wars* story.

Some games require you to be in the park. However, when you can't be in your happy place, test your knowledge of Disney trivia and other fun activities at home.

GRAND HOLIDAYS

Christmas Delights From Coast to Coast

H ome for the holidays has special meaning for those who consider the Disney parks "home." Beginning in mid-November and lasting through the first week in January, Disneyland and Walt Disney World celebrate the holidays in a myriad of merry ways. The resorts are festive, too, and don't require a hotel stay or park admission to enjoy the spirit of the season. Grab your hot chocolate and get ready for a grand holiday on either side of the country.

Disney's Grand Floridian Resort & Spa is one of the most resplendent hotels at Walt Disney World. With its Victorian decor and five-story lobby featuring stained glass domes, the Grand Floridian becomes a spectacular winter wonderland during the holidays. When it comes to the decorations, matching the design with the Victorian time period is top of mind for the designers (and the trees are themed to "The Twelve Days of Christmas"!). For more than 20 years, the life-size gingerbread house—standing at more than 14 feet (4 m) tall and with room inside for six adults—has been one of the most popular seasonal displays. Guests have the opportunity to watch it being assembled over the course of a week, which is truly a spectacle. For those ambitious bakers who want to (wink) replicate this at home, the pastry chefs provide the recipe as part of the display. When the holiday season ends, so does the gingerbread house. Since sustainability is always in mind at Walt Disney World, the baked components are removed, and the structural components—with their sugary residue—are repurposed to feed the local bee colonies during the winter months when food sources are harder to find.

RECIPE FOR SUCCESS

Ever wonder what the ingredients are for the Grand Floridian's gingerbread house? Dough not worry. Yule learn here: 1,050 pounds (476 kg) of honey, 140 pints (66 L) of egg whites, 600 pounds (272 kg) of powdered sugar, 700 pounds (318 kg) of chocolate, 800 pounds (363 kg) of flour, and 35 pounds (16 kg) of spices.

OPPOSITE: Holidays at Disney are magical, right down to the special treats.

PAGES 92-3: The gingerbread house in the Grand Floridian stands at 14 feet (4 m) tall.

Disney's Grand Californian Hotel & Spa is the first Disney resort located within a theme park. With craftsman-style architecture, the interior design is inspired by the Monterey pines and redwood forests along the California coastline. It's also home to one of the most welcoming and cozy spots at any Disney hotel: the massive stone fireplace and inviting rocking chairs. Although not as imposing, the Grand Californian's gingerbread house is just as impressive. And in California, the creation varies from year to year. Part of the fun is seeing what the chefs created and, on special days, getting the opportunity to meet them and ask questions. The lobby easily accommodates a towering tree decked with arts and crafts–style ornaments such as woodcut art and mica lanterns. It's a favorite spot for family photos.

The Candlelight Processional is a Christmastime tradition started by Walt in 1958. It is celebrated at Disneyland and EPCOT. ∎

THE MERRY IN MERRY-GO-ROUND

We often associate gingerbread with houses, but Disney's Beach Club Resort turns the holiday treat into a colorful carousel. Entirely made of edible materials, the carousel has been presented since 2000. The theme changes year to year, as do the horses' names. The gingerbread carousel is strictly for show, but it's big enough for four small children to ride. For further amusement, there is one Hidden Mickey for each year of the carousel's existence. Can you find them all?

HOLIDAY HAPPENINGS

Every Disney park in the world celebrates the holidays. The festivities, decor, landscaping, seasonal treats, Disney characters decked out in holiday garb, exclusive merchandise, parades, towering trees—and spirit!—are unparalleled. Attractions receive special overlays, including one of Walt's originals at Disneyland, "it's a small world." The ride gets a completely new look with dolls adorned in winter finery and special songs such as "Jingle Shells." Disney Cruise Line offers Very Merrytime Cruises. And Adventures by Disney will take you to the Christmas markets in the heart of Europe. Whether on a day trip or a vacation, you'll find a Disney way to celebrate the holidays.

A: Main Street, U.S.A. in the Magic Kingdom gets a festive overlay—right down to Cinderella Castle. B: You don't have to be home for the holidays—set sail with Mickey, Minnie, Goofy, Pluto, Chip, and Dale on a Disney holiday cruise. C: It's all in the details—including this edible Rudolph—when it comes to the gingerbread house display at Disney's Grand Floridian Resort & Spa. D: You might spot Donald Duck—all covered in snow—in the lobby of Disney's Contemporary Resort. E: Enjoy a festive performance aboard the *Disney Dream* on a holiday cruise. F: Nana from *Peter Pan* (1953) comes to life—in chocolate!—in the holiday displays at the BoardWalk Bakery. G: Holiday decorations at Disney's Contemporary Resort include a chocolate Christmas tree. H: *Ho, ho, ho!* Santa rode his merry sleigh down Main Street, U.S.A. in the Magic Kingdom during the 2014 Christmas Parade.

A

D

B

E

F

G

H

PIN-WORTHY MOMENTS

Collect and Swap Pins Throughout the Disney Parks

Pin trading has been an Olympics custom dating back to the first Summer Games in Athens, Greece, in 1896. The tradition is as much about swapping stories as it is about swapping enamel. With this as an inspiration, Walt Disney World started their pin-trading program in 1999. Disneyland followed in 2000, and Disneyland Paris joined in on the fun in 2001.

Whether you're at the parks, in a resort, or on a cruise, pin trading is ubiquitous. It takes very little to get going—just one pin. Pins are sold at gift shops in the parks and resorts, Downtown Disney, Disney Springs, shopDisney, and independent online sellers. It doesn't matter if pins are new or used; they're Disney's most fun currency. There are pins for nearly every Disney character, attraction, and park, plus limited editions, special editions, and exclusives. Lanyards are the typical way to display them, and there are starter sets for those who want, well, a head start. No experience is required, either. Approach *anyone* wearing pins, including cast members, and ask if they want to trade. Cast members like to barter, too, and unlike some discerning guests, they never turn down the opportunity to discuss a trade.

Although lanyards are classic, there are also vests, sashes, purses, messenger bags, and special ears on which you can display your pins. Wherever you are in the parks, check the daily schedule for pin-trading "meet-ups" in places such as Frontierland at Disneyland and outside the parks at Downtown Disney and Disney Springs. ■

DISNEY PINS 101

With an ever changing selection of more than 60,000 pins, understanding the different kinds can be daunting. They are sorted by color categories (priced lowest to highest) and described with acronyms such as LE (Limited Edition), LR (Limited Release), and OE (Open Edition). Rare ones include AP (Artist Proof): The stamp on the back indicates how many were produced—usually 24 or fewer.

Pin trading is a Disney rite of passage.

MEET MICKEY AND MINNIE

Spend Quality Time With the Iconic Mouse Duo

Walt famously said, "It was all started by a mouse." He had made cartoons with other lead characters, but it wasn't until he lost Oswald the Lucky Rabbit in a 1928 business dispute that he was pressed to create something new. Walt, the eternal optimist, didn't waste any time. He took out his sketch pad and started working on a new character, a mouse. The first name he chose was Mortimer; however, his wife didn't care for it. According to legend, it was Lillian Disney who proposed the name Mickey—and Walt agreed: Mickey Mouse was born!

Later that year, Mickey first appeared in an animated short—the first with synchronized sound—called *Steamboat Willie*. In it, Mickey is a mischievous deckhand who goes to great lengths to impress Minnie, also making her debut. The premiere was November 18, 1928. This date is therefore the "birthday" of Mickey and Minnie.

Mickey is not unlike any other celebrity. Seeing him on television or in a movie is fine, waving to him in a parade is gratifying, but meeting him in person is priceless.

Millions are eager to meet him, as well as Minnie, and special venues offer this unique opportunity in the parks worldwide.

Beginning with Disneyland, Mickey's Toontown home features mementos such as the broomstick from 1940's *Fantasia* (in which he starred as the Sorcerer's Apprentice) and a photo with his pal Walt. Adjacent is Mickey's Movie

MORE FROM WALT

"When people laugh at Mickey Mouse it is because he's so human; and that is the secret of his popularity," said Walt. "All we ever intended for him or expected of him was that he should continue to make people everywhere chuckle with him and at him."

OPPOSITE: Meet Mickey and Minnie in the parks—and don't forget to ask for their autographs!

PAGES 100-101: Your favorite pals may stop by your table during Breakfast à la Art with Mickey & Friends at Topolino's Terrace—Flavors of the Riviera in Disney's Riviera Resort.

Barn, where guests can pose for pictures and share a hug with Mickey backstage. Mickey also has a home at Tokyo Disneyland, where fans have an opportunity to take photos with him while he takes a break from filming at his studio.

When Mickey visits the Magic Kingdom, he can be found backstage at Town Square Theater on Main Street, U.S.A. Situated in his rehearsal room, and with some of his magic tricks surrounding him, he may pull a rabbit out of his hat before saying "cheese" with his guests.

At Disneyland Paris, Magician Mickey invites you to his dressing room to look at some of his props, including the feather that gave Dumbo the confidence to fly. He might even perform a card trick before taking photos with his fans.

The Gardens of Imagination—created specifically for Shanghai Disneyland and the first land in any Disney park designed as a botanical oasis—is the newest location to meet Mickey Mouse. The queue is a colorful gallery of portraits depicting Mickey's impressive career. At the end, you'll find Mickey waiting for you inside a diorama with Enchanted Storybook Castle in the background.

WHO IS MICKEY?

"Walt is Mickey. If Mickey is good, it is because Walt is good. Every characteristic of Mickey's from the lift of his eye-brow to his delightful swagger is Walt's own. Mickey is not a mouse; he is Walt Disney." —*Overland Monthly,* October 1933

OPPOSITE: Join Mickey and Minnie in paradise at Aulani, A Disney Resort & Spa.

ABOVE: Walk ashore at Castaway Cay and be blown away by who's waiting to greet you on the sand.

And let's not forget Minnie! A star in her own right, she co-starred with Mickey in his first cartoon, *Plane Crazy* (released in 1929), and made her theatrical debut with her sweetheart in *Steamboat Willie* in 1928. She presides (with Mickey) in Red Carpet Dreams at Disney's Hollywood Studios. Wearing one of her sparkly red-carpet gowns, her smile lights up the room. And she's ready to light up your day, too.

All the world's a stage for Mickey and Minnie, so you'll have other opportunities to meet them. Character dining (see page 268) is a fun way to interact with your favorite characters as they go from table to table. On board Disney cruises, nautical Mickey and Minnie host the official send-off party as the ship sets sail. Or say "Aloha!" to the lovable duo at Aulani Resort in Hawai'i. ∎

MOVIE MAGIC

Watch Your Favorite Film in Style

Thanks to Disney+ we can watch our favorite Disney movies—past and present—at home. But nothing beats the communal experience of watching with an audience. Add to that the glamour of a fully restored Hollywood theater and you have the El Capitan, or fondly, "El Cap." The theater debuted in 1926—and was restored to the style of that time period in 1989, with many of the original design elements. And just as the classic movie palaces of yesteryear had organs, the "Mightiest of Mighty Wurlitzers," with more than 2,500 pipes, rises from below the stage and is played for audiences prior to showtime, making the experience truly memorable. Many Disney and Pixar movies premiere at the El Capitan. Look for special events offered here by D23 (page 76). Complete the yesteryear experience before or after a screening at the Ghirardelli Soda Fountain and Chocolate Shop. Located on Hollywood's Walk of Fame and adjacent to the theater, it offers a full menu of ice cream classics such as sundaes, shakes, and cones, plus hot chocolate and sweet treats. There's also a wide array of Disney gifts, collectibles, and souvenirs.

Bring your favorite Disney plushie, blanket, and snacks outdoors to join fellow guests for a complimentary Movie Under the Stars at Walt Disney World Resort hotels. Available on select evenings, the movies are shown poolside, beachside, on the grass near the lobby, and even on the football field at Disney's All-Star Sports Resort. Fort Wilderness Resort & Campground has its own outdoor venue (page 29). Inclement weather moves the event indoors at most locations. Disneyland Resort hotels also offer nighttime movie-viewing experiences. ■

Hollywood's El Capitan Theatre is the place to be for Disney film premieres.

CHAPTER TWO

ADVENTURE IS A WONDERFUL THING

Activities for the Tame and Daring

The lobby of the Hollywood Tower Hotel at Disney's Hollywood Studios (page 144) is almost as frightful as the elevator ride to the top.

A KISS GOODNIGHT

Attend a One-of-a-Kind Nighttime Spectacular

Walt loved fireworks ever since he was a young boy in Marceline. His hometown put on a fireworks display every Fourth of July, which is why Disneyland has a nightly spectacle behind Sleeping Beauty Castle.

Songwriter and Disney Legend Richard Sherman (who composed many Disney classics with his brother Robert, including "A Spoonful of Sugar," "I Wan'na Be Like You," and "Winnie the Pooh") recalls that Walt referred to the fireworks tradition as a "kiss goodnight"—his way of thanking guests for coming to his park. One evening, he and his wife ran into Walt at Disneyland on their way out of the park. "Walt, we just had to thank you for the most wonderful time today," commented Richard. "In fact, when the fireworks started and the music was playing and Tinker Bell flew across the sky, I was so overcome with happy emotions that I was crying. Walt looked me straight in the eye and with a little smile said, 'You know, I do that every time . . . Now drive home carefully.' With a fond wink, Walt headed for his apartment above the fire station."

Walt Disney World: Book a table at California Grill atop Disney's Contemporary Resort for dinner. Even if your meal ends hours before dusk, you may return to the 15th-floor restaurant for a dazzling view of the nighttime spectacular at the Magic Kingdom. Nearby, the waterfront cabins at Copper Creek Villas & Cabins at Disney's Wilderness Lodge have a breathtaking vista from within their private screened porches. Fireworks Dessert Parties take place on the Tomorrowland Terrace with a wonderful view of Cinderella Castle, great seats, and tasty treats. Or embark on an iconic ferryboat with Ferrytale Fireworks: A Sparkling Dessert Cruise on the Seven Seas Lagoon;

OPPOSITE: Say *bonne nuit* to Disneyland Paris with a dazzling display set behind Sleeping Beauty Castle.

PAGES 110-11: Fireworks and dessert? You really can have it all on Ferrytale Fireworks: A Sparkling Dessert Cruise on the Seven Seas Lagoon.

sip, savor, and sail as you watch the fireworks light up the sky.

Disneyland Paris: Disney Illuminations is the nightly pièce de résistance here, with breathtaking projections on Sleeping Beauty Castle accompanied by captivating music and Parisian pyrotechnics. In November only, Mickey's Magical Fireworks has a "reel" special effect. As the show commences, a black-and-white lighting illusion beams, simulating the flicker of an old-fashioned movie. Mickey's whistle from *Steamboat Willie* (1928) packs an emotional wallop. It is, after all, the cartoon that started it all.

Tokyo Disneyland and Tokyo DisneySea: Disney Light the Night is a fireworks display that bursts across the skies of both parks. Familiar Disney songs from films such as *Beauty and the Beast* (1991), *The Lion King* (1994), and *Tangled* (2010) are featured; however, it's "Live the Magic," the theme written for Disneyland's 60th celebration, that tugs at the heartstrings.

Shanghai Disneyland: Watch ILLUMINATE: A Nighttime Celebration from the Disneytown Imagination Terrace. Told in seven sequences, the story follows your favorite princesses, heroes, and friends on a story of light and dreams. The

YOU CAN FLY, YOU CAN FLY, YOU CAN FLY!

Tinker Bell started flying from the top of the Matterhorn and over Sleeping Beauty Castle prior to the Fantasy in the Sky fireworks show at Disneyland in 1961. She took her first flight over the Magic Kingdom in 1985.

exclusive experience takes place on a standing platform offering panoramic views of Disney's newest park.

Hong Kong Disneyland: The Castle of Magical Dreams is the canvas for this brand-new nighttime spectacular celebrating "endless magic." Guests are taken on a journey of life's cherished moments told the way Disney does best—with characters, music, and lots of special effects.

Disneyland: Sleeping Beauty Castle has been the setting for fireworks since they began at Disneyland in 1956 with Fantasy in the Sky. However, there are nighttime spectaculars in other lands. Fantasmic! at Disneyland takes place on Tom Sawyer Island with Mickey, magical lighting, film clips, and fire effects, plus boatloads of cherished characters on the *Mark Twain* and *Columbia*. The show uses mist—and there may be some in your eyes, too. Over at Disney California Adventure Park, World of Color is a water wonder, featuring 1,200 programmable fountains, 36 fire-emitting cannons, and 28 high-definition projectors. ∎

OPPOSITE: The fireworks at Tomorrowland in Disneyland are out of this world.

ABOVE: Say goodnight to the Magic Kingdom with the most magical of celebrations.

NIGHTTIME SPECTACULARS

A Disney tradition since 1956, fireworks have evolved from pyrotechnics in the sky to full-on multimedia productions. Now, technology is making things magical even for those who cannot be in the parks: virtual fireworks! Guests staying at Walt Disney World resorts can stream a prerecorded performance on demand from the comfort of their hotel rooms. For those who'd like to have dinner, ride an attraction, or just have a relaxing day at "home" during the show, this is for you. Families with little children will appreciate watching well before bedtime.

A: Take in the ultimate fireworks display from Main Street, U.S.A. in the Magic Kingdom. B: The red torii gate in Japan at EPCOT frames the stunning fireworks show on World Showcase Lagoon. C. Ghostly dancers are projection-mapped onto Cinderella Castle during the Halloween fireworks in the Magic Kingdom. D: Harmonious at EPCOT brings music, fireworks, lights, and water into perfect sync. E: Your boat ride comes with a show on Ferrytale Fireworks: A Sparkling Dessert Cruise. F: Get a one-of-a-kind view of fireworks as a guest of Disney's Grand Floridian Resort & Spa. G: Fireworks burst above the Matterhorn Bobsleds in Tomorrowland at Disneyland. H: A show of two Walt favorites: A Disneyland fireworks display bursts above the *Mark Twain* riverboat.

A

D

WATER, WATER EVERYWHERE

A Catamaran Ride and Private Snorkel Adventure

Hawai'i is one of the most remote island chains in the world—and Disney is there, too.

At Aulani, A Disney Resort & Spa, located on the west coast of O'ahu, there are two fun ways to enjoy the Pacific. A sail-and-snorkel excursion offered through Aulani Resort's Holoholo Desk is a four-hour ocean adventure on a 65-foot (20-m) sailing vessel. As you cruise, you may spot dolphins, sea turtles, and, from December through April, humpback whales! A guide takes you into the water to help spot the colorful creatures of the sea. Then you'll have time to relax and enjoy O'ahu's sun. Lunch, transportation, and an afternoon full of memories are included.

Fish are an important part of Hawaiian culture, and to see them up close, you don't need to be scuba certified or even wade into the sea at all. Disney's Aulani Resort offers Rainbow Reef, a unique snorkeling experience especially for its guests. A private 166,000-gallon (630,000-L) saltwater lagoon sits adjacent to the beach and is home to nearly 50 different species of native reef fish. You can snorkel in this oasis, and the resort even provides special gear (a regulator and flotation device) to make it easy and fun. Aulani Resort aquarists are also available to help identify fish and share stories of Hawaiian ecosystems to help fully immerse you in nature's beauty.

With its two large observation windows, Rainbow Reef can be enjoyed without even changing into a swimsuit. ∎

Aulani Resort's Rainbow Reef offers a private snorkeling experience among hundreds of reef fish.

MEDAL OF HONOR

Make Haste to Race for a *run*Disney Medal

Whether you are a regular runner, jogger, or brisk walker, "every mile is magic" with *run*Disney.

Fun is first and foremost. As Jeff Galloway, training expert for *run*Disney and former Olympian, advises, "I've not found any experience which offers the high level of satisfaction, accomplishment, and self-respect as one receives from finishing a marathon—at any speed."

If you're like Hercules and willing to "Go the Distance," Walt Disney World Resort hosts several *run*Disney events for all fitness levels and age groups. Costumes and ears are welcome for all. Beginning well before dawn, you'll have a rare opportunity to traverse the parks before they open to guests. Along the way are photo ops, character meet and greets, and entertainment to motivate and inspire. The reward—besides bragging rights—is one of the most highly sought-after Disney collectibles: a one-of-a-kind commemorative medal.

Or medals.

Make a resolution to start the new year with the Walt Disney World Marathon Weekend in January. It features four races: 5K, 10K, half marathon or 13.1 miles (21 km), and full marathon or 26.2 miles (42 km). The Goofy Challenge combines the half and the full. For the ambitious, the Dopey Challenge is a doozy: all four races—48.6 miles (78 km) total—over four consecutive days. Finishers receive a medal for each race, the Goofy Challenge medal, plus the special Dopey Challenge medal.

February brings the Disney Princess Half Marathon Weekend. Run in a tiara and represent your favorite heroine. If you're interested in extra bling, the

FEAT OF THE FEET

Colorado runner Brittany Charboneau set a record in 2022 by winning all four of the *run*Disney races at the Walt Disney World Marathon Weekend. No runner had won the Dopey Challenge (5K, 10K, half, and full marathon on four consecutive days) in the event's nearly 30-year history. Charboneau dressed in costumes daily and fueled herself with Disney cookies.

OPPOSITE: Ready, set, eat! Racers line up to run for the finish line—and the snacks—at the Disney Wine & Dine 10K.

PAGES 120–21: Runners have the parks to themselves as they race through Walt Disney World.

Disney Fairy Tale Challenge may be for you. Complete the Disney Princess Enchanted 10K and the Disney Princess Half Marathon to earn a challenge medal worthy of a queen or king.

The Wine & Dine Half Marathon Weekend in November—which culminates with a postrace party at the EPCOT International Food & Wine Festival—also offers the Disney Two Course Challenge: 19.3 miles (31 km) when you combine the 10K with the half marathon. Finish both and earn an additional shiny challenge medal.

The *run*Disney Springtime Surprise Weekend—held in April—began in 2022. The first year's events included a nighttime run and scavenger hunt in Disney's Animal Kingdom, the Race for the Taste 10K inspired by *Ratatouille* (2007), and the not-too-terrifying Twilight Zone Tower of Terror 10-miler. But no two years will look alike. Take on all three running events (race distances may change year to year) to see what surprises are in store for you—and earn your challenge medal.

Want to add some hardware to your collection? Be sure to plan ahead, as *run*Disney events sell out quickly. ∎

SET YOURSELF UP TO SUCCEED

There's no need to be daunted by the distance of a *run*Disney race. Achieve your goals with former Olympian and *run*Disney trainer Jeff Galloway. The training is free. Whether you're a marathon veteran or have just mustered the courage for your first 5K, simply download the training program suited for you at *rundisney .com*, tie your shoelaces, and go.

THE ULTIMATE FUN RUN

W e know that Disney is fun. The *run*Disney events are fun, too—and there's no reason you should miss out, even if you can't make it to Walt Disney World. All *run*Disney events—any 5K, 10K, and even the Dopey Challenge—have a virtual extension where you can run at home and earn an event medal. Or take part in the *run*Disney Virtual Series, held every summer. To participate, tackle up to three 5K runs at home—at your own pace and on your own schedule.

A: Talk about a photo finish: Nothing beats running down Main Street, U.S.A. in the Magic Kingdom. B: Race across the drawbridge of Cinderella Castle and into New Fantasyland. C: A hard-earned medal on Castaway Cay means you deserve a little R & R on the sand—or cruise ship—after crossing the finish line. D: Medals won't be the only accessory during the race—*run*Disney runners often dress as their favorite Disney characters. E: You might spot characters cheering you on from the sidelines. F: Can you get them all? Earn your yearly Castaway Cay medal and hang it with pride. G: Mickey and Minnie make the ultimate cheerleaders during *run*Disney events. H: You'll find magic and fantasy from start to finish at a *run*Disney event.

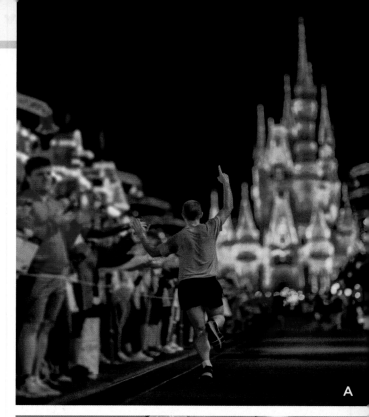

A

D

B

C

E

F

G

H

ADVENTURE IN ADVENTURELAND

Join an interactive hunt for secret treasures hidden throughout Adventureland. You may have been walking past them all this time—now it's your turn to discover them all.

There's no fee to participate in A Pirate's Adventure: Treasures of the Seven Seas. Mateys of all ages report to the Crow's Nest. Once enlisted, you'll be given a Magical Talisman (or use your Magic Band). Before you leave the enlistment quarters, you'll be handed a treasure map and given your first clue to get you started.

Go on five separate quests to help Captain Jack Sparrow recover all the items scattered throughout Adventureland. Marauders mind the instructions—go only where commanded as you search for the cleverly camouflaged markers. When you unlock them using your Magical Talisman, you'll be rewarded with real-life magic and surprises. But beware! What looked like an inanimate object will come alive. Heed the warnings and advice before continuing the treasure hunt.

Complete all five missions and you'll get a sixth card signed by Captain Jack himself. Missions have no time limit. Need some grub and grog? You can stop and restart at your convenience throughout the day.

NOT YOUR LAZY-DAYS VACATION

Golf, Bike, and Play on the Coast of South Carolina

D isney's Hilton Head Island Resort is a Disney Vacation Club resort located on the scenic coast of South Carolina, only a five-hour drive from Walt Disney World. The resort is themed as a 1940s hunting and fishing lodge, which is appropriate considering how many sports and recreational activities are available here.

Hilton Head Island is a top 10 American destination for golfers and is renowned for its beautiful and challenging courses. The Professional Golfers' Association Heritage Classic is played at Sea Pines Resort's Harbour Town Golf Links, and you can play there, too. The resort can arrange a tee time at Sea Pines, or any of the nearby courses that give the island its golf credentials.

Tennis anyone? The island's more than 300 courts include hard courts, clay courts, and lit courts. Private lessons are available by request.

Looking for something more leisurely? Bike along hundreds of miles of scenic bike trails, including the 1.25-mile (2-km) path that leads to Disney's Beach House, a marine-themed clubhouse situated on the Atlantic Ocean beachfront and the perfect place to relax with the family.

Back at the main resort, there's bocce, basketball, shuffleboard, table tennis, and a putting green. For nature enthusiasts, take a guided walk, go on an adventure to Pinckney Island National Wildlife Refuge, or take a boat ride to meet the friendly dolphins in Broad Creek.

Whether you're tame or daring, you'll find something to suit your fancy. ■

Discover the beauty of South Carolina's coast, marshes, and golf courses at Disney's Hilton Head Island Resort.

WALT'S BARN

In the early 1950s, Walt built a personal railroad in the backyard of his Los Angeles home. He named it the Carolwood Pacific Railroad (CPRR) as an homage to both the Central Pacific Railroad that he so admired and the street he lived on—Carolwood Drive, in Holmby Hills, California. He numbered his *Lilly Belle* locomotive 173, the same number as the Central Pacific 173. Using a technique called forced perspective, he also constructed a scaled-down version of the barn that sat on the Disney family farm in Marceline, Missouri (page 84). Inside, he could remotely control the switches on the train's track. It provided a respite, a place he could go to relax after a long day at the studio. An accomplished woodworker, Walt tinkered there, built miniatures and model trains, and occasionally entertained friends.

The barn's historical significance is even greater: It's where Walt worked on his plans for Disneyland, and so it's considered by many to be the birthplace of Imagineering. A portmanteau of *imagination* and *engineers*, "Imagineers" is the term Disney uses to refer to engineers, designers, architects, artists, and others who helped Walt build Disneyland, as well as those who continue to design Disney parks and experiences around the world today.

When Walt's childhood home sold years after he passed away, his daughter Diane was determined to save her father's Carolwood barn. In 1999, the Disney family moved it to the Los Angeles Live Steamers Railroad Museum in Griffith Park, of which Walt was a founding member.

Operated by the nonprofit Carolwood Foundation, Walt's Barn preserves his railroad legacy and celebrates his passion for all things trains. It contains memorabilia, including the workbenches he built, his tools, the old-fashioned telephone with a line that went directly to the house, rare photographs, gifts from friends and others who shared his hobby, and the original switch panel.

OPPOSITE: Walt Disney's Carolwood Barn was moved to Griffith Park and is part of the Los Angeles Live Steamers Railroad Museum.

PAGES 130-31: Walt used his barn, steps away from his home in Holmby Hills, California, to build working trains for what he called the Carolwood Pacific Railroad.

Walt's Combine—train speak for a car that combines passengers and freight—is on display. Called Retlaw 1 ("Walter" spelled backward and the name of his private corporation), it's similar to the one on the Missouri Pacific train Walt worked on as a 15-year-old newsboy. Young Walt often took breaks from selling sundries in the combine car—which sits closest to the locomotive—of the Missouri Pacific. Though a combine car wasn't practical for Disneyland's railroad (the luggage and freight area took up potential seating space for guests), Walt included one anyway. The combine car ran as part of the park's railroad until 1974. Later, it found its way to the care of the Carolwood Foundation. The car sits adjacent to an exhibit that showcases both railroading and Disneyland history, including Walt's railroading influences and time lines beginning with his father, Elias, in the mid-1800s and ending with Walt's passing in 1966.

Be sure to find Disney Legend Ollie Johnston's station. Ollie, known for his work on characters such as Thumper from *Bambi* (1942), Mr. Smee from *Peter Pan* (1953), and Baloo from *The Jungle Book* (1967), was also a railroad enthusiast and one of Walt's "Nine Old Men," an affectionate nickname Walt coined for his key animators.

Walt's Barn is open for free to the public on the third Sunday of each month from 11 a.m. to 3 p.m. Parking is complimentary and donations are gladly accepted. ■

EPCOT

SEA-ZE THE DAY

Spend Your Day Under the Sea

The exterior of The Seas with Nemo & Friends pavilion at EPCOT in Walt Disney World is a treat unto itself with its larger-than-life characters Marlin, Dory, and Gill, plus the seagulls who occasionally bark "Mine, mine, mine!" And our favorite clownfish, of course. It's also the entrance to The Seas with Nemo & Friends attraction. Guests board "clamobiles" and descend beneath the waves, where they encounter Bruce, leader of the support group Fish-Friendly Sharks; dodge jellyfish; and ride the Eastern Australian Current (EAC) with Crush.

However, the real adventure is inside: the stunning 5.7-million-gallon (21.5-million-L) saltwater Caribbean Coral Reef Aquarium. Host to 4,000 sea creatures representing 60 aquatic species, it's the second largest aquarium in America and one of the largest human-made ocean environments on the planet. Spot sea turtles, unicorn tangs, dolphins, rays, and sharks. Go to the second floor's Observation Deck and surround yourself with marine life.

Don't miss the majesty of the manatees. The large water-dwelling creatures are mesmerizing. And just like you, they're only visiting. Disney's animal care experts provide ill and injured manatees with the stable, controlled environment they need to make a recovery; the goal is to return the manatees to the wild after the appropriate amount of rest and rehabilitation when possible.

Forgetful Dory needs your help to find her friends. On a complimentary self-guided scavenger hunt throughout the aquarium, follow a map through

OPPOSITE: The 5.7-million-gallon (21.5-million-L) Caribbean Coral Reef Aquarium is one of the largest human-made ocean environments on the planet and is home to more than 4,000 sea creatures.

PAGES 134-5: Have a lively conversation with your favorite totally tubular sea turtle at Turtle Talk with Crush in World Nature at EPCOT.

the pavilion, solving clues and collecting stickers. Look for Mr. Ray and get schooled along the way. Learn fun facts about amazing ocean animals as you navigate among the many exhibits and displays.

Little dudes and dudettes will get seriously stoked with Turtle Talk with Crush. Sit in front of the attraction as the totally tubular shell-ebrity swims right up to you. Communicating directly with the audience using a hydrophone, Crush answers questions and shoots the breeze. The conversation is in real time, interactive, and improvised. Every show is different. Whoa!

For a different type of aquatic experience, make a reservation at the under-the-sea-themed Coral Reef Restaurant. The lunch and dinner menus feature ocean specialties along with land-based and kid-friendly items. The floor-to-ceiling window showcases the reef and a variety of sea life, putting on a show with your meal.

Come and *sea* it all for yourself! ■

NEW BEGINNINGS

The Living Seas pavilion opened in 1986 to house the Coral Reef Restaurant and The Living Seas attraction. Aboard a Sea Cab vehicle, guests journeyed deep underwater to Seabase Alpha. The 2003 film *Finding Nemo* inspired two new attractions: Turtle Talk with Crush and The Seas with Nemo & Friends. The reimagined pavilion opened in 2006.

HIDDEN MICKEY HUNT

What started as an inside joke among Imagineers—"hiding" the three-circle form or silhouette of Mickey Mouse's head—has evolved into one of the most popular unofficial fan experiences. Finding Hidden Mickeys in the Disney parks, attractions, resorts, restaurants, and cruise ships delights all ages. The rules are simple: There are no rules. Have fun on your scavenger hunt!

Spotting something hiding in plain sight, much like a chameleon, can be a challenge. For those looking for clues or helpful hints, ask a cast member. They will be more than happy to oblige.

Mickey & Minnie's Runaway Railway in Disney's Hollywood Studios is the first ride-through attraction at any Disney park worldwide starring Mickey Mouse and friends. It's also the site, appropriately so, of the most Hidden Mickeys at any of the four Walt Disney World Resort parks. Keep your eyes peeled from the moment you enter the queue until you disembark the train.

Spoiler alert: The largest Hidden Mickeys aren't seen in an attraction, park, ship, or resort. They are visible only from the air—and it might take a cruise around Google Earth to find them. At Walt Disney World, one solar array—sporting 48,000 panels—is in the shape of Mickey. Located near EPCOT, the five megawatt solar farm produces enough energy to power the equivalent of 1,000 homes. At Disney's Animal Kingdom, Expedition Everest's circular outer tracks form Mickey's ears, and the mountain is in the shape of his head.

Oh, boy!

IT'S A PIRATE'S LIFE FOR ME

Find Gold on Pirates of the Caribbean: Battle for the Sunken Treasure

When Pirates of the Caribbean was being developed by Walt for Disneyland, he told his Imagineers to think bigger than the Audio-Animatronics figures successes they had with the Carousel of Progress and Great Moments with Mr. Lincoln at the 1964–1965 New York World's Fair: "That's fine for Mach 1. But I'm thinking Mach 3."

At Shanghai Disneyland, Imagineers honor the original attraction while catapulting it to Mach 10. Pirates of the Caribbean: Battle for the Sunken Treasure is like nothing else at any Disney park in the world.

With cutting-edge Audio-Animatronics figures, state-of-the-art media, and a unique ride system, this is as close to being inside a scene of the iconic film franchise as anyone can get.

In the vast, abandoned fortress, guests set sail on the ultimate adventure. The action begins with Captain Jack Sparrow transforming from a skeleton to his mortal pirate self. Disney Legend Hans Zimmer's *Pirates of the Caribbean* theme pulses as the boat "plunges" underwater. Sunken ships abound. The Kraken awakens. And ethereal mermaids defy the escapades ahead.

As piles of treasure come into view, so does Davy Jones, acutely aware that his archrival is in his midst. Suddenly, the doomed vessels rise to the surface and the battle ensues. Swashbuckling takes on a whole new level as Captain Jack and Davy engage in a spectacular sword fight, providing a derring-do finale before one final surprise—but we won't spoil the ending for you. ∎

Davy Jones stakes claim to the sunken treasure in the Pirates of the Caribbean attraction in Shanghai Disneyland.

BE BRAVE IN SCOTLAND

Set Sail for a Taste of Merida's Homeland

Pixar's official web page for *Brave* (2012) teases, "Since ancient times, stories of epic battles and mystical legends have been passed through the generations across the rugged and mysterious Highlands of Scotland. A new tale joins the lore when the courageous Merida confronts tradition and challenges destiny to change her fate."

For lucky lads and lasses aboard the Disney cruise departing from Dover, England, a "brave" adventure awaits!

After the Disney ship docks in Greenock, Scotland, guests will travel to Edinburgh, which sits atop extinct volcanoes and bluffs. Following a brief tour of historic monuments in medieval Old Town and New Town, it's on to the famed Edinburgh Castle. Tour the former home of Scottish kings and queens, and gain inspiration for the activity that awaits. Children ages five and older will learn about family coats of arms and their symbolism. Then, led by Disney Cruise Line youth activities counselors, each child will create a shield—or targe—the perfect memento from this exclusive excursion. While the kids are making memories, parents are free to explore the castle on their own.

Everyone comes back together before the highlight of the afternoon: an audience with Disney royalty—Merida. Meet the fiery red-haired legend and take a photo with her before returning to your motor coach.

Looking for a fun fact to impress your fellow Disney cruise passengers? Castle DunBroch is the *first* castle to appear in a Pixar movie. ∎

MEET MERIDA

Merida is a Scottish heroine. Born to royalty, she's a passionate and headstrong teenager. An excellent archer, horsewoman, and sword fighter, she's most comfortable in the outdoors. Merida is on a quest, declaring, "There are those that say fate is something beyond our command. That destiny is not our own. But I know better. Our fate lives within us. You only have to be brave enough to see it."

Live like Merida with authentic bagpipe performances and a tour of the fiery redhead's home country.

A PERFORMANCE IN PARADISE

Celebrate Hawaiian History at Aulani, A Disney Resort & Spa

KA WA'A—a Lū'au takes place at Aulani Resort's Hālāwai Lawn. The performance is an exploration of Hawaiian history that will enchant the entire family. Preshow demonstrations include taro pounding—the process of preserving taro, a starchy root vegetable and a mainstay for those wayfarers who sailed for months on a canoe. Then it's all ears for a special welcome chant and a three-course meal featuring island fish and other local fare, including decadent desserts. There are also options for children (*keiki* in Hawaiian).

No luau would be complete without entertainment. And who does entertainment better than Disney? Get ready for dancing with the stars as Mickey and Minnie demonstrate the official "Aulani hula." Then give it a go yourself! The magical production also features the stories of Hawai'i brought to life through singing, storytelling, drumming, and a fire dancing finale.

There are two packages for KA WA'A—a Lū'au: general and preferred. Both include a lei and all beverages, alcoholic and nonalcoholic. Preferred guests also get a photo, early check-in, and priority seating. KA WA'A—a Lū'au offers American Sign Language interpretation by request; please call 14 days in advance for this service.

Don't miss this enchanting journey through Hawaiian history. Aloha! ∎

Dancers celebrate Hawaiian traditions during performances at KA WA'A—a Lū'au.

FOR THRILL SEEKERS

Great Drops and Stomach-Turning Loops Across the Disney Parks

Disney certainly knows how to enchant and entertain. They also know how to thrill. For daring park visitors—those with mighty mettle and strong stomachs—here are the top-notch attractions for adrenaline rushes:

Rock 'n' Roller Coaster Starring Aerosmith: When this white-knuckler opened at Disney's Hollywood Studios in 1999, Aerosmith was one of the hottest bands in the world. After a preshow at G-Force Records, it's life in the fast lane as you speed past Hollywood landmarks in a super-stretch limo. The band has invited you to their concert, and you race to get there in time. On the way, encounter traffic jams, two rollover loops, and one corkscrew. Each vehicle broadcasts different Aerosmith hits on the 125-speaker, 24-subwoofer, 32,000-watt audio system.

The Twilight Zone Tower of Terror: This attraction based on the 1960s television series *The Twilight Zone* is located on Gower Street and Sunset Boulevard at Disney's Hollywood Studios. Heed the admonition that you may be able to check in, but you can't check out. Explore the decaying hotel before encountering host Rod Serling, who explains the fateful Halloween night in 1939 when unfortunate hotel guests were riding the hotel's elevator just as a lightning storm struck. The attraction climaxes with a 13-floor drop down an abandoned service elevator shaft, but not before you glimpse the park below and preview how far you'll fall. Next stop, the Twilight Zone!

Mission: SPACE: Before civilian space travel on Blue Origin or Virgin Galactic, EPCOT had astronaut training for the X-2 Deep Space Shuttle at the International Space Training Center. Today, there are two simulator

RESISTANCE RECRUITS

Welcome to the Cause . . . and the most massive, interactive, immersive, and epic attraction in the galaxy. Star Wars: Rise of the Resistance puts you at the heart of the action (and as a prisoner of the First Order). The scale and scope of the escapade is staggering. The nearly 20-minute, multiple-ride-system experience is a thrilling, first-of-its-kind adventure!

OPPOSITE: Enter if you dare—The Twilight Zone Tower of Terror drops elevator riders 13 stories: the ultimate thrill.

PAGES 146-7: Hang on tight! The Rock 'n' Roller Coaster Starring Aerosmith blasts off at superfast speeds.

adventures to choose from: Orange Mission to Mars is intense and uses a centrifuge that spins and tilts to simulate the speed and g-force of a spacecraft launch and reentry. Orbiting Earth on the Green Mission is gentler and family-friendly.

Guardians of the Galaxy: Cosmic Rewind: Imagineers developed an all-new type of roller coaster—the Omnicoaster—for this EPCOT attraction. It rotates 360 degrees, enabling riders to focus on the action and help the Guardians save the galaxy. It features the first ever reverse launch on a Disney coaster and is one of the longest indoor coasters in the world. Rocket, Groot, Gamora, Drax, and Star-Lord are eager to see you.

TRON: Tron Lightcycle Power Run at Shanghai Disneyland is being joined by TRON Lightcycle / Run in the Magic Kingdom at Walt Disney World. Based on the eponymous franchise, riders board a train of two-wheeled Lightcycles for a thrilling race through the Grid and digital frontier. The semi-enclosed attraction features a dramatic "curved wave" canopy, known as the Upload Conduit, which gives both riders and guests on the ground riveting views. ■

PIXAR COASTERS

Set in Andy's oversize backyard at Toy Story Land in Disney's Hollywood Studios, Slinky Dog's springy coils stretch to the limit as you bend around twisting turns and drops on Slinky Dog Dash. Over at Disney California Adventure, try to catch Jack-Jack on the Incredicoaster. From the standing start, take off to the enclosed tunnels and special effects—you're sure to be super-fied!

HOLE IN ONE

Work on Your Swing at Fantasia Gardens and Winter Summerland Mini Golf

For many families planning their vacation at Walt Disney World, certain days are set aside to enjoy activities outside of the parks. Fun is in the fore-cast when you putt your way through four 18-hole miniature golf courses. Two of the courses are inspired by one of the most highly regarded Disney films; the others take you on a madcap adventure where an unlikely scenario becomes reality.

The first two courses pay homage to *Fantasia*. The innovative film premiered in 1940, with an orchestral score conducted by Leopold Stokowski. At Fantasia Gardens and Fairways Miniature Golf, located near EPCOT and Disney's Hollywood Studios, it's more about luck and whimsy than skill. Putt through musical notes, piano keys, pop-up mushrooms, spinning snowflakes, crocodile mouths, a spinning hippo in a tutu, and around Sorcerer Mickey—his buckets of water come into play—on the 18th hole.

Disney's Winter Summerland Miniature Golf Course is a very merry vacation! As the story goes, Santa was flying back to the North Pole one Christmas Eve. As he passed over Orlando and the vacation capital of the world, it occurred to him that he might create an off-season destination for his elves. As exciting as that was, the elves and Santa were conflicted. Some elves welcomed a warm summer environment; others preferred the familiarity of the North Pole's freezing temperatures. They compromised, building a sand course to represent the sunny beaches of Florida called "Summer," where you can "Deck the Balls" past sand castles and surfboards, and a snow course called "Winter," where you putt your way to the "North Hole." ■

Two 18-hole mini golf courses at Fantasia Gardens and Fairways Miniature Golf, which opened in 1996, celebrate the movie *Fantasia* (1940).

DISNEY'S ANIMAL KINGDOM THEME PARK

BE LIKE RUSSELL

The Wilderness Must Be Explored

Become a Wilderness Explorer just like Russell, the perky sidekick from *Up* (2009), who was eager to earn his "assist the elderly" badge by helping cranky widower Carl. And you can do it without traveling to Paradise Falls in a balloon-powered house.

The Wilderness Explorers program at Disney's Animal Kingdom is the big idea of two committed groups: the cast members from Disney's Animals, Science and Environment (ASE) department and the Walt Disney Imagineers. The ASE cast members worked with Walt Disney Imagineering to further the park's mission to bring awareness to conservation and protecting the planet. The Imagineers took that concept and partnered with Pixar and its artists to bring *Up* to life through badges, artwork, and design.

The result is one of the most fun, educational, and interactive attractions at any of the Disney parks. Follow in Russell's footsteps as you take nature-themed challenges on a self-guided adventure.

To begin, take the pledge: "A Wilderness Explorer is a friend to all, be it plants or fish or tiny mole."

Pick up your complimentary handbook from any Wilderness Explorers station to get started. There are three easy steps to exploring: Use the map to find one of the badge locations in the park. Follow the instructions on each page to complete the activity. Find a Troop Leader, easily identified by their uniform and orange satchel, and collect your badge.

As you earn badges, learn about insects, botany, flamingos, ecology, safaris, habitats, recycling, animal nutrition, hiking, veterinary medicine, forestry, bats, tracking, gorillas, conservation, Mount Everest, birding, fossils,

OPPOSITE: Troop leaders and rangers will guide you through nature prompts— like animal hand signals and calls—so you can earn Wilderness Explorer badges.

PAGES 152-3: Russell and Dug may greet you at the Wilderness Explorers Club House.

dinosaurs, tigers—did you know they are one of the most endangered creatures in the world?—and animal calls.

Speaking of calls, there is a Wilderness Explorer Call badge. Troop Leaders at Wilderness Explorers Headquarters will teach you the official call and hand signals, just as Russell did in *Up:* "The wilderness must be explored! Caw! Caw! RAWR!" Don't be shy. Russell isn't. Try your call with fellow Wilderness Explorers throughout the day.

Earn all the badges and become a Senior Wilderness Explorer. Never fear: You can go at your own pace; if you cannot complete all the badges, bring your handbook back on your next visit and keep exploring!

There's no badge on the line, but can you identify who is the current Chief of the Wilderness Explorers at Disney's Animal Kingdom? The correct answer is Pete Docter, chief creative officer at Pixar Animation Studios. He was bestowed the honor as the director of *Up*. Pete also directed other iconic Pixar films including *Monsters, Inc.* (2001), *Inside Out* (2015), and *Soul* (2020). ∎

CHEW ON THIS

Wilderness Explorers know that all animals have special diets based on their needs. People don't eat hay for dinner, just as hippos don't eat macaroni and cheese. The wrong food can make us both sick. To earn your Animal Nutrition badge, you'll need to learn all about animals and the diets that help them thrive. Wilderness Explorers promise *never* to feed an animal in the wild.

THE MENEHUNE ADVENTURE TRAIL

Menehune—the mischievous "little people" of Hawai'i—are known for their magical powers and for working at night. You may wake up to find a bridge or canoe in progress, and chances are it's the Menehune who are responsible.

Evidence of the Menehune is scattered throughout Aulani Resort—in its landscaping, in the lobby, under tables, and nestled under rocks. And Aulani Resort invites you to learn more about Hawai'i and its legends on an interactive treasure hunt.

As you meander along the Menehune Adventure Trail with a tablet provided by the resort's Pau Hana community hall, solve riddles and follow the clues. Answer correctly and you'll be rewarded with the scenery coming to life!

The adventure is complimentary for resort guests, and it's a wonderful way to spend time as a family.

WALT'S EARLY YEARS IN LOS ANGELES

When Walt came to Los Angeles in 1923, bankrupt and with plans for a fresh start, he rented a room from his uncle Robert in Los Angeles. When he didn't get hired as a live-action movie director—his ambition at the time—he went back to what he knew: cartoons. Walt bought a used camera and set his sights on a new "studio." Uncle Robert rented Walt his small wooden garage for an additional dollar a week. Using spare lumber, Walt built an animation bench and set to work on gag reels he sold to a local theater owner.

Soon thereafter, Walt and his brother Roy signed a contract to produce the *Alice Comedies*, and the Disney Brothers Cartoon Studio was born. It was apparent, however, that they would need more room. Walt found a temporary office a few blocks from Uncle Robert on Kingswell Avenue in the rear of a realtor's building. They outgrew that space quickly, moving next door in 1924; 4649 Kingswell is considered the first legitimate location for the Disney Brothers Cartoon Studio. A few years later, the Disney brothers established a new studio on Hyperion Avenue, the site where Mickey Mouse was born and *Snow White and the Seven Dwarfs* (1937) was produced. With all the success came the need for even more production space. In 1940, they moved permanently to the state-of-the-art Walt Disney Studios in Burbank.

You can still visit these sites, among others, on a Walt-filled tour around Los Angeles. The garage adjacent to Uncle Robert's house was slated to be demolished until a group called Friends of Disney saved it. Unable to find a

OPPOSITE: **The Disney Brothers Cartoon Studio, founded on October 16, 1923, was where Walt (right) worked with artists and Disney Legends such as Ub Iwerks (left) and Rollin "Ham" Hamilton (center).**

PAGES 158-9: **After several years in Los Angeles, Walt (pictured) and Roy moved their company to Burbank, California, which is still the home of The Walt Disney Studios.**

location to display the landmark, Friends of Disney had the house dismantled and rebuilt in a permanent location at the Stanley Ranch Museum & Historical Village with the Garden Grove Historical Society.

The Walt Disney Studio on Hyperion Avenue has been razed and is currently the site of a Gelson's supermarket; still, history buffs may enjoy visiting the site (2701 Hyperion Avenue) and imagining the early glory days of animation.

And, of course, the current Walt Disney Studios comprise several blocks in Burbank. To get a look inside where the magic is made, join D23: The Official Disney Fan Club to take a tour (page 76).

Beyond the studios, there are other markers of Walt's early years in Hollywood, most significantly, Walt's first home in Los Angeles. Uncle Robert's craftsman bungalow is now designated as a historical landmark and is held within the Los Angeles Conservancy. Although tours are not offered, the home is intact and easily visible from the street. The 1914 craftsman house is located at 4406 Kingswell Avenue. ∎

MORE FROM WALT

"I take great pride in the artistic development of cartoons. Our characters are made to go through emotions which a few short years ago would have seemed impossible to secure with a cartoon character. Some of the action produced in the finished cartoon of today is more graceful than anything possible for a human to do."

TAKE THE PLUNGE

Summit Plummet: The Ultimate Water Park Thrill

This near-vertical drop is for hard-core thrill seekers! Summit Plummet is the most extreme attraction at Disney's Blizzard Beach Water Park. In fact, it may be one of the most extreme attractions in Walt Disney World Resort.

Designed to resemble a ski jump, the waterslide sits atop Mount Gushmore (Disney loves a good pun). It's one of the fastest free-fall body slides in the world. As if that's not enough to entice—or terrify—the plunge is 360 feet (110 m). As a cast member prepares you for the very rapid descent at the edge of the slide, you won't be able to see where you are going, the drop is so steep. After passing through a dark tunnel and hurtling down a straightaway, you'll splash to a heart-pounding stop.

For those less daring, yet still seeking a legitimate thrill, there is the Slush Gusher. This high-speed, snowbanked body slide is designed to resemble the excitement of gushing water and features two dips in a 90-foot (27-m) drop.

In keeping with the mountain theme, a chairlift takes guests to the top of Mount Gushmore. If you'd like to summit on your own two feet, take the stairs.

Still too much? Those who are tamer can choose from other slides, including the Downhill Double Dipper. After waiting for the starting gates to open, race an opponent on side-by-side waterslides as you both travel 50 feet (15 m) downhill in inner tubes.

You can also check out Teamboat Springs (cue Mickey's whistle), a family-style white-water raft ride. ■

Summit Plummet at Disney's Blizzard Beach is the third tallest free-fall waterslide in the world, sending riders down 360 feet (110 m).

TAKE A WALK ON THE WILD SIDE

The Sea Turtle Night Walk and Conservation at Disney's Vero Beach Resort

Every summer on Florida beaches, tens of thousands of threatened and endangered sea turtles emerge from the Atlantic Ocean to nest. During the ancient ritual, the mommy sea turtles dig holes a few feet deep with their rear flippers. After filling their nests with eggs, they cover them with sand before returning to the sea. It takes some planning to witness this wonder of the natural world, so why not leave all the details to Disney?

The Disney Vacation Club at Vero Beach Resort sits down the coast from the Archie Carr National Wildlife Refuge, home to three species of nesting turtles. The Disney Conservation Team Wildlife estimates that, since 2003, nearly 1.4 million sea turtles have hatched on the beaches near the resort.

You can engage in the resort's community science efforts in a few ways: Guests of Disney's Vero Beach Resort can join one of Team Wildlife's sea turtle specialists each morning of sea turtle nesting season (April through October) as they search for nesting activity from the night before. Sometimes you'll see a freshly laid nest. Or you might see that a nest has recently hatched! During nesting season, you're also invited to weekly presentations about the sea turtle conservation program at which you can see sea turtle skull models and a model of a life-size hatchling.

Looking for something extra special? Each year on the last Saturday of July, Team Wildlife joins forces with the Sea Turtle Conservancy to offer

RIPPED FROM THE SCREEN

"You've got serious thrill issues, dude . . . awesome!" —Crush the sea turtle from *Finding Nemo* (2003)

OPPOSITE: Search for nesting sea turtles along Florida's Treasure Coast with the help of the Disney Conservation Team Wildlife's sea turtle specialists.

PAGES 164-5: The Disney Conservation Team Wildlife works to protect the sea turtles on Vero Beach's shores, safeguarding nests and only allowing visitors to observe from a distance.

Tour de Turtles—a sea turtle migration marathon. Two female sea turtles are outfitted with satellite transmitters so scientists can track their movements as they leave the beach and head to their foraging grounds. Watch as the mama turtles make their way into the ocean from the resort's beach.

Seeking a daytime adventure instead? Join the Disney Conservation Team Wildlife on Florida's famous Treasure Coast. The conservation team helps care for the three species of endangered sea turtles located there: loggerheads, greens, and leatherbacks. (For the record, Crush is a green turtle who prefers tropical waters.) During the outing you may see a freshly laid nest or, depending on the time of the year, hatchling turtles clambering across the dunes and into the waiting ocean.

Or join "Turtle Tracks," an education program that teaches children about sea turtle biology and conservation. ∎

HOME AWAY FROM HOME

The Seas with Nemo & Friends at EPCOT is for entertainment, education, and inspiration. It's also a rehabilitation center for Florida sea turtles that have been injured by boat strikes, illness, or entanglement. Disney's Animals, Science and Environment team has nursed more than 300 endangered sea turtles back to health there. Once recovered, they're released into the ocean again, sometimes fitted with transmitters that allow scientists to track their movements and better understand their conservation needs.

THE PEAK EXPERIENCE

Ride the Mountains Across the Disney Parks

Have you seen the "I am just here for the mountains" T-shirts in the parks? Riding the Disney mountains around the world has become an unofficial challenge. Here are a few that made the list: **Space Mountain** opened at Walt Disney World in 1975 and Disneyland in 1977, long after Walt passed away. However, Imagineer and Disney Legend John Hench recalls Walt suggesting Space Mountain as early as 1964: "Walt wanted to build a roller coaster–style ride, but in the *dark*, which no one had done before . . ." Walt's wishes for the attraction were realized after he passed away. Once you take off, you can't see the tracks, making it difficult to anticipate the drops and tight turns. Adding to the thrill—and sense of speed—are the outer space effects and shooting stars. All mountains are more than 180 feet (55 m) high and 300 feet (90 m) in diameter. Despite their similarities, each of the other Space Mountain attractions has its own special twists—and the Space Mountain in Disneyland Paris stands out as particularly unique.

Big Thunder Mountain Railroad premiered at Disneyland in 1979 and later at Walt Disney World (1980), Tokyo Disneyland (1987), and Disneyland Paris (1992). Imagineer and Disney Legend Tony Baxter was first inspired by the scenery at Bryce Canyon National Park in Utah; the subsequent three attractions resemble Arizona's Monument Valley. Although it may be tamer than many of the Disney roller coaster–style attractions, it is rich in Old West detail and storytelling. After boarding the train, you climb through a dark tunnel and then the journey through caverns, sandstone gorges, and abandoned mine shafts ensues. For Disney park history buffs, check out the Big Thunder

OPPOSITE: **Legend has it that eerie incidents took place in the mine of Big Thunder Mountain Railroad in Disneyland—so keep an eye out for a goat chewing dynamite and one colossal dinosaur skeleton.**

PAGES 168-9: **Expedition Everest's track is also the location of a Hidden Mickey (page 136).**

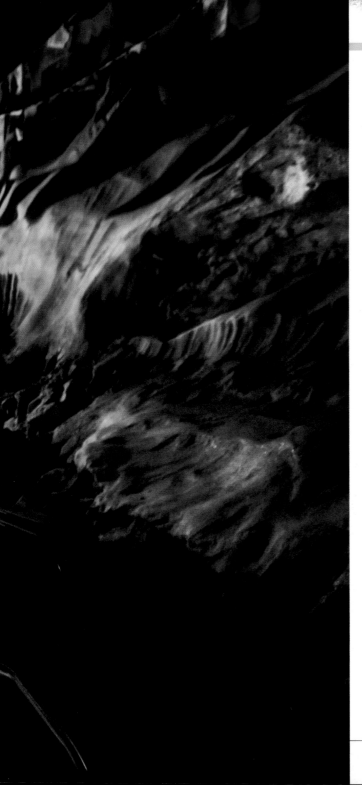

model built by Baxter on display at the Disneyland Hotel's Frontier Tower.

Seven Dwarfs Mine Train is based on Walt's full-length animated film *Snow White and the Seven Dwarfs* (1937) and is an attraction the whole family can enjoy. Entertaining queues are one of the many innovations Walt brought to theme parks. While you're waiting for your mine train adventure—whistling optional—look for magic in the jewels and glowing stones, and a note from Doc, too. Once you've boarded, the swaying coaster takes you into an age-old mountain, through the diamond mine where the Seven Dwarfs dig for glittering treasures, and alongside Snow White's cottage. Heigh-Ho, Heigh-Ho, it's off to this attraction you go!

Splash Mountain premiered at Disneyland in 1989 and was the first flume ride created for a Disney park. Walt Disney World and Tokyo Disneyland followed in 1992. Whichever Splash Mountain you ride, you're guaranteed to get wet, not just splashed.

Expedition Everest—Legend of the Forbidden Mountain debuted at Walt Disney World in 2006. At just under 200 feet (61 m), the mountain is one of the tallest mountains in Florida—natural or otherwise. The legend of the Yeti, believed for thousands of years in the Himalaya, sets the tone for the tale ahead. Once boarded, the train takes you on a steep ascent to the "top of the world." After encountering a twisted track that goes nowhere, you're hurtled backward into darkness and within sight of the mythical beast that stands more than 20 feet (6 m) tall. ■

SET SAIL

Take to the Seven Seas on a Boating Adventure

Walt Disney World is surrounded by water, and most Disney resorts have marinas that offer a wide range of adventures. Many marinas offer guided catch-and-release outings that let everyone get in on the fun. The bass fishing excursions are two or four hours. All equipment is included, and experience is not required. If you're an ambitious angler, the tournament-style NITRO bass fishing boat is an option for up to three guests.

Chartered fireworks cruises depart nightly from the marinas at Disney's Yacht Club Resort, Contemporary Resort, Polynesian Village Resort, Grand Floridian Resort & Spa, Fort Wilderness Resort & Campground, and Wilderness Lodge. The 25-foot (7.6-m) boat is operated by a captain, can accommodate up to 10 guests, and includes assorted snacks and soft drinks while you watch the show with spectacular views of Cinderella Castle.

Want to captain your own adventure? Pick up your motorized boat at one of several marinas. Sun Tracker Pontoons can seat up to 10 passengers. Go at your own pace and cruise the scenic lakes, lagoons, and inlets. Pass by the theme parks or dock at a hotel for lunch or dinner. It's all up to you and your crew. Drivers must be at least 18 years old and present a valid driver's license, state-issued ID, or military ID.

If you prefer people-powered versus motorized—and you are a guest of the Walt Disney World Swan and Dolphin Resort—book a swan boat, so named to reflect the swan shape and whimsy of the white watercraft. Using pedals, just like a bicycle, you can glide around Crescent Lake at your own pace. Kids get giddy with the independence of navigating their own route. Delightful for all ages. ■

Take a cruise on the Seven Seas Lagoon: Water taxis and ferries sail to and from the Magic Kingdom.

THE (MIGHTY) KING OF SAFARIS

Rhinos, Elephants, Hippos, Oh My! A Chance to Get Up Close to the Animal Kingdom

Disney's Animal Kingdom Theme Park, which opened in 1998, is dedicated and committed to animals and conservation. It entertains guests as much as it educates. At 500 acres (200 ha), it's Disney's largest theme park, which is needed as the creatures from Africa, Asia, and beyond need lots of room to roam. The following up close and personal experiences at Animal Kingdom are exceptional:

The three-hour **Wild Africa Trek** brings you to Safi River Valley—an environment that resembles the animals' untamed home turf in Africa. The tour includes walking along paths and over rope bridges (with harnesses) and riding in rugged safari vehicles where you can observe crocodiles, rhinos, hippos, and more in the open savanna. This experience also includes African-themed snacks such as kachumbari (Kenyan tomato and onion salad), sundried tomato hummus, and prosciutto and mozzarella. Stay immersed in what you're doing and seeing and don't worry about finding your camera or phone at the perfect moment; a professional photographer accompanies your tour and will capture all the magical memories.

Kilimanjaro Safaris are offered daily to all Animal Kingdom Theme Park guests. The guided expedition in an open-air vehicle takes you through the Harambe Wildlife Reserve, 110 acres (44 ha) of savannas, wetlands, and forest landscapes. More than 30 species, including mandrills, cheetahs, giraffes,

SOFA SAFARI

Skip a trip to the parks and get unprecedented behind-the-scenes access to the creatures and the animal experts who care for them. From your living room, stream *Magic of Disney's Animal Kingdom* on Disney+.

OPPOSITE: Kilimanjaro Safaris takes you on an 18-minute expedition through the Harambe Wildlife Reserve, home to 34 species.

PAGES 174-5: On the VIP Wild Africa Trek, you'll have close encounters with exotic African wildlife.

lions, and hyenas, are waiting for you to spot them in their natural environment.

Up Close with Rhinos offers a truly unique encounter with white rhinoceroses, the second largest land animal on Earth! Meet members of a "crash," the term used for a herd of the heavy-horned mammals. The Animal Care Team will take you on a 60-minute guided backstage tour where you will be one of the few to encounter these massive creatures up close. You'll learn how they are cared for, their biology, and their behavior. For the safety of the animals, cameras are not allowed on this tour. Guests must be four years of age or older.

Caring for Giants explores the elephant herd at Disney's Animal Kingdom, the park's largest inhabitants. This is your chance to observe these brilliant and sentient souls from as close as 80 to 100 feet (24 to 30 m) away. Animal educators conduct the behind-the-scenes experience; they'll detail the elephants' day-to-day routines and provide you with fascinating facts, such as how these giant pachyderms go through six sets of molars in a lifetime! You'll also get a chance to learn about different conservation efforts that Disney supports that help preserve elephants in their homelands around the world. Guests must be four years of age or older.

MORE FROM WALT

"What I have learned from the animal world, and what anyone will learn who studies it, is a renewed sense of kinship with the earth and all its inhabitants."

Starlight Safari is an immersive safari adventure that resembles what you might experience on a nighttime drive through an African game reserve. As the sun sets, the savanna awakens! To be sure you can see all that can be seen, night vision goggles are provided. While aboard your open-sided safari vehicle, you'll observe zebras, gazelles, antelope, ostriches, and other exotic African species. This one-hour nighttime expedition at Disney's Animal Kingdom Lodge is open to all Walt Disney World guests eight years of age or older.

Disney's Animal Kingdom Lodge After Dark—Night Vision is a favorite for all ages. This experience is not a safari. However, it is an adventure. From the perimeters of the savanna, observe the nighttime behaviors of giraffes, bongos, zebras, wildebeests, impalas, African spoonbills, and the once endangered blue crane, the national bird of South Africa, through the green glow of night vision goggles. The experience is complimentary for Disney's Animal Kingdom Lodge guests. ∎

CHAPTER THREE

A WHOLE NEW WORLD

Vacations and Excursions Around the Globe

The *Disney Magic* docks at Castaway Cay, Disney's private island accessed only by cruise-goers.

ALASKA THREE WAYS

Family-Friendly Journeys to the Last Frontier

Three exclusive and exciting excursions can be experienced only on a Disney cruise to Alaska. These adventures may be reason enough to choose this seven-night cruise from Vancouver aboard the *Disney Wonder*.

Liarsville Gold Rush Trail Camp & Salmon Bake Featuring Exclusive Disney Character Experience: The port of call is Skagway; however, the excursion is in Liarsville. The town got its name during the Klondike gold rush from journalists who were sent there to cover the news and cooked up some half-baked stories. Which brings us to salmon. It's wild, caught in Alaska, and the feature of the all-you-can-eat buffet. You'll want to work up an appetite first. Begin with a performance in the Hippodrome, featuring puppets, dance hall girls, and "sourdoughs"—not the bread, but rather a term for miners who spent their winters in Alaska. Next, a scavenger hunt will help you find the equipment you'll need to pan for gold. You're guaranteed a nugget.

Disney characters might join in on all the fun, making it an adventure only Disney can do!

Disney Exclusive Glacier Dog Musher for a Day: An ice field in Juneau offers a once-in-a-lifetime opportunity to take the reins of a dogsled and yell "Hike!" just like mushers of the Iditarod, the annual long-distance sled dog race run in early March from Anchorage to Nome. But first, meet the crew of a mushing team and their sled dogs. Tour their camp and its

BEHIND THE LENS

Walt's first nature film was set in Alaska. He hired Al and Elma Milotte to shoot a documentary. His intention was to give audiences an experience they couldn't have in real life. After reviewing the initial footage, he said simply, "More seals." *Seal Island* was the first *True-Life Adventures* featurette (1948) and went on to win an Academy Award.

OPPOSITE: Special characters might surprise you on excursions.

PAGES 182-3: Paddle the waters of Alaska off the coast of Juneau.

living quarters, cookhouse, kennel, and veterinary clinic. Prepare for your mushing adventure by preparing your dog team with a hearty meal, coat brushing, and welfare check. Then it's off to the "races" across the snowcapped Norris Glacier.

Alaska Family Fun and Exclusive Lumberjack Show: Alaska is a land with many traditions. This day offering gives a glimpse into a few of them. In Saxman Native Village, learn about totem poles—their meaning and mystique—from initial concept to finished product. Then view the largest collection of totem poles in Ketchikan. Visit the Southeast Alaska Discovery Center and then walk to the nearby Great Alaskan Lumberjack Show, where Southeast Alaska's logging history comes to life. Get in on all the *axe*-ion by witnessing world-champion athletes competing in a number of thrilling displays of strength and agility, from logrolling to tree climbing. And axe throwing, of course. This unique, Disney-exclusive show offers kid-friendly activities that are fun for the entire family. Plaid shirts optional. ■

MORE FROM WALT

Walt and his youngest daughter, Sharon, then 10, went on a three-week Alaska adventure in 1947. It turned out to be a wonderful daddy-daughter bonding experience. There was one precarious landing in Candle and much of the trip was rugged, but they loved it. On this trip Walt had the opportunity to see the breathtaking scenery and charming seals of Alaska in real life. *Seal Island* was released one year later.

GREAT APE ESCAPE

See the Gorillas of Uganda and Rwanda

Set off on a once-in-a-lifetime journey to Uganda and Rwanda to encounter chimpanzees and mountain gorillas in the wild, with a National Geographic expert at your side.

The Great Apes of Uganda and Rwanda expedition brings you to the Chimpanzee Sanctuary on Ngamba Island in Uganda. Established in association with the Jane Goodall Institute, it's a habitat for rescued and orphaned chimpanzees. Goodall, the world-renowned anthropologist and humanitarian, inspires the mission to save chimpanzees from extinction: In 1900, an estimated one million chimpanzees lived in the wild; today, there are fewer than 340,000.

Fly from Entebbe to Kasese en route to Kibale National Park. Learn about the conservation efforts of the Kibale Chimpanzee Project from field director and National Geographic grantee Emily Otali before heading into Bigodi Wetland Sanctuary to look for primates such as red and blue monkeys, black-and-white colobus monkeys, and the rare l'Hoest's monkeys.

Two days of the expedition are spent in Queen Elizabeth National Park. Named for Queen Elizabeth after her 1954 visit, this is the most popular savanna park in Uganda and home to the biggest variety of large mammals in the country. It's also a birder's paradise with more than 600 species in the park. While there, go on safari to look for elephants, lions, and Ugandan kobs before setting off on an afternoon wildlife cruise.

Next is Bwindi Impenetrable National Park. This location is so stunning that it served as inspiration for the jungle in *Tarzan* (1999). Roughly half of the world's remaining mountain gorillas live here. Venture to the forest to sit with

MEET GINO

Animal Kingdom is home to many gorillas, but one stands out: silverback Gino, the oldest in the park—he turned 41 in 2021. Gino is often seen being playful and engaging with the people and animals around him. He interacts with children through the viewing panel of his habitat and loves to be the center of attention. See Gino on the Gorilla Falls Exploration Trail.

OPPOSITE: Trek into the forests of Rwanda to witness mountain gorillas in the wild.

PAGES 186-7: Seek primates and other wildlife on treks through various forests and wetlands.

these sentient creatures—from a distance—who are among the planet's most endangered species.

A private villa overlooking Rwanda's spectacular volcanoes welcomes you for even more adventure. Meet experts at the Dian Fossey Gorilla Fund's Karisoke Research Center. Fossey, author of *Gorillas in the Mist*, realized that to study gorilla behavior, she must learn to recognize individual gorillas, which required the gorillas to become accustomed to her presence. Today, you can trek to see the gorilla family groups she researched for 18 years in Volcanoes National Park.

Take an excursion in the park, guided by wildlife biologist and National Geographic grantee Deogratias Tuyisingize, to search for endangered golden monkeys, known for their unique character and distinctive yellow patches.

Travelers should be physically fit and prepared for multiple hours of walking or hiking over uneven terrain on some days. While tracking primates, guests will trek up to eight hours through thick jungle at elevations that may reach 10,000 feet (3,000 m). ∎

A HELPING HAND

Based on the trusting relationships Gino developed with Disney's world-class animal care experts, his laid-back attitude allows them to brush his teeth and perform cardiac ultrasounds (heart disease is one of the leading killers of his species). His agreeable temperament also allows keepers to train him and develop important techniques that benefit gorillas in managed care around the world.

ADVENTURES BY DISNEY

INTO THE NILE

An Exclusive Egyptian Getaway

E gypt and epic go hand in hand. Explore the ancient country for 10 days, beginning in the capital city, Cairo, which juxtaposes the old with the new. A private tour of the esteemed Egyptian Museum is on the agenda. View the Pharaoh Tutankhamun collection and other treasures covering 7,000 years of history with an Egyptologist (one of whom will be guiding you throughout your journey). Junior Adventurers will be engaged with their own King Tut activities.

Have lunch in Al-Azhar Park, an oasis known for intersecting waterways, sunken gardens, and bold Islamic geometric design; the Project for Public Spaces lists it as one of the world's 60 great public spaces. An excursion to Old Cairo includes stops at the Saladin Citadel of Cairo, a UNESCO World Heritage site, and the Mosque of Muhammad Ali.

Visit one of the seven wonders of the ancient world, the Great Pyramid of Giza, and enjoy VIP access to the Great Sphinx of Giza. This mythical part-human, part-lion creature was carved from a single piece of limestone and is one of the world's largest sculptures. You'll enjoy a private and uncrowded opportunity to see the Sphinx, an experience typically only available to visiting dignitaries.

After a traditional Egyptian dinner, visit a souk—or marketplace—that dates back to the 14th century. This landmark of Old Cairo is an excellent example of medieval Islamic architecture.

The Nile River beckons you! Cruise on the famous waterway for three days. Disembark for excursions, including a visit to the Temple of Isis at Philae, which

OPPOSITE: Tour the grandeur of Egypt's ancient history, including the Sphinx.

PAGES 190-91: The guided group family tour of Egypt includes visits to the pyramids and other ancient treasures, including the Karnak temple complex.

honors the goddess Isis, an important figure known as the giver of life. You can also take a walk through the world's largest ancient religious site, the Karnak temple complex, with its avenues of sphinxes and nearly 100-foot-tall (30-m) towering obelisk. Have the Luxor Temple all to yourself on a private, after-hours tour of the site believed to be where several Egyptian kings were crowned.

Take flight to Sharm el-Sheikh. Located on the shores of the Red Sea, the Coral Sea Sensatori resort in Sharm el-Sheikh overlooks Ras Muhammad National Park. A private yacht brings you to the southern end of the Sinai Peninsula the following morning for a guided snorkeling experience among coral reefs. Then enjoy a private beachside dinner themed for the local Bedouin nomads who call Middle Eastern deserts home.

Your Egyptian vacation concludes in Cairo with a farewell dinner shared with your fellow adventurers. ∎

NO PASSPORT REQUIRED

If you can't make it to Egypt, an attraction called Soarin' Around the World features the Great Pyramids. The experience, played in a 180-degree IMAX digital projection dome, is available at EPCOT, Disney California Adventure, and Shanghai Disneyland. Gliding over the oldest of the seven wonders of the ancient world on a flight motion simulator, you have the opportunity to experience their majesty without packing a suitcase.

WALT DISNEY'S BIRTHPLACE

Walt Disney was born on the second floor of a modest Chicago home in 1901. Completed in 1893, the house was built by his parents, Flora and Elias. Flora said about her design, "There's nothing mysterious about drawing up plans for a house. And a woman ought to know about making it livable." Elias, who learned his carpentry skills during a stint on the Union Pacific, built the 18-by-28-foot (5.5-by-8.5-m) wood cottage to his wife's specifications, painting it white with blue trim.

Elias would go on to construct other homes in Chicago. He also volunteered to build a church for the congregation where he and his family worshipped. Elias had become friends with the preacher, Walter Parr, and occasionally delivered the sermon at St. Paul's Congregational Church when the preacher was on vacation. This friendship is also how Walt got his name. With both their wives pregnant at the same time, Elias and Walter made a pact: If boys were born, they would name them for each other. Walter Elias Disney was born on December 5, 1901. (Elias Parr followed.)

Walt joined big brothers Herbert, Raymond, and Roy, who would go on to be his lifelong business partner. Little sister Ruth joined the family in 1903. The longest time that all seven members of the Disney family lived together was in this Chicago home, from Ruth's birth until 1906.

With five children and a neighborhood that was becoming increasingly dangerous at the time, Elias told his wife they needed to move out of the city. He felt a rural area would be best to raise his young family with

OPPOSITE: The Disney family left their modest home in Chicago when Walt was four and Roy was 12.

PAGES 194-5: Walter Elias Disney was born in Chicago on December 5, 1901.

wholesome values. After considering Colorado and Alabama, Elias purchased a farm in Marceline, Missouri (see page 84). In 1911, less than five years later, the Disney family relocated to Kansas City. There, Walt discovered and became enamored with vaudeville and movies.

It's also where he rose daily at 3:30 a.m. to deliver newspapers for his father's distributorship. A clever homage to this history is "hidden" at Disney California Adventure. Look carefully at the "Storytellers" statue: In Walt's back pocket is a folded Kansas City newspaper, and "Marceline" is stamped on the bottom of his shoe.

In 1917, Walt and his family returned to Chicago. Walt attended McKinley High School as a freshman. He concentrated on drawing and photography and served as an artist on the school magazine, *The Voice*. He also attended the Academy of Fine Arts in the evenings.

Walt's first childhood home, at the corner of Tripp Avenue and Palmer Street just outside downtown Chicago, has changed hands many times over the years. Renovations and upgrades significantly altered the original dwelling, but it has been faithfully restored and will become an interactive museum. The founders explain their vision: "Our dream is that The Walt Disney Birthplace becomes a portal to new approaches in early childhood development and helps to inspire future Walts and Roys." ∎

CRUISE INTO DISNEY HISTORY

Follow in Walt's Footsteps on River Cruises of the Seine and Rhine

The Seine River Cruise begins and ends in one of Walt's favorite cities—Paris. His first trip there, however, was not a vacation; it was during his post–World War I service with the Red Cross Ambulance Corps and motor pool as a 16-year-old (he had to lie about his age to join). On this eight-day river cruise, you'll take part in his story with a visit to Le Havre, where Walt landed on December 4, 1918, the day before he turned 17. The day's itinerary also includes Normandy and Omaha Beach, one of the sites of the D-Day invasion. Visit Pointe du Hoc, the location where U.S. Army Rangers scaled the 100-foot (30-m) cliffs and engaged the enemy.

There is still more fodder here for Disney history buffs: Walt's French ancestors hailed from a small seaside village on the Normandy coast called Isigny-sur-Mer. The name d'Isigny would later be anglicized to the Disney surname.

Other excursions include the picturesque town of Honfleur, which inspired the works of artists Gustave Courbet, Eugène Boudin, and Claude Monet. A walking tour of Rouen sheds light on the Vikings and Joan of Arc. In Giverny, tour the beautifully restored 19th-century home where Monet lived from 1883 until his death in 1926. Art buffs will enjoy the Museum of Impressionism, where Monet's art—and art by those he influenced—is on display. Explore Château de Malmaison, the castle of Napoleon and Josephine Bonaparte. Roam the suburbs where 19th-century artists Paul Cézanne, Camille Pissarro, Jean-Baptiste-Camille Corot, and Vincent van Gogh lived and painted.

ALL ABOARD

Adventures by Disney River Cruises feature a different type of vessel than those built for ocean travel. The ships are specifically designed to navigate European rivers. Passengers are accommodated in luxury that includes the Chef's Table specialty restaurant.

OPPOSITE: Cruise the Seine River through beautiful Rouen in Normandy, France.

PAGES 198-9: Sail by—or visit—historical castles, such as Stolzenfels Castle near Koblenz, Germany, on the Adventures by Disney Rhine River cruise.

Sail back to Paris and say "Au revoir," which literally means "until we see each other again" in French.

Basel, Switzerland, is the starting point for the eight-day Rhine River Cruise. Thrill seekers may consider a real-life Matterhorn-type adventure on an alpine toboggan ride. Walt was chiefly inspired to build his Matterhorn Bobsleds attraction after a visit to the *Third Man on the Mountain* (1959) set in Switzerland. When asked why there were holes in his Disneyland mountain, he famously quipped: "Because it's a Swiss mountain."

You may prefer seeing the Black Forest, known for its beautiful highlands and pastoral farms. The scenic woods were also an inspiration for Beast's castle in *Beauty and the Beast* (1991).

The following day, more Disneyland history is on the Strasbourg itinerary. Its Cathedral of Notre Dame, completed in 1439, is home to an astronomical clock. Created in 1843, the clock intrigued Walt on his visit to France in 1935. Besotted by the animated figures, he sketched it and even tried to climb the tower to see how it worked. And he

MORE FROM WALT

Walt returned to Le Havre in August 1961 for the filming of *Bon Voyage!* (1962). The comedy is about a family that sets sail on their dream vacation to France, only to experience unforeseen adventures. The film starred Fred MacMurray, one of Walt's favorite actors and a friend. He also starred in *The Absent-Minded Professor* (1961), *Son of Flubber* (1963), and *The Happiest Millionaire* (1967), among other films for Walt Disney Productions.

brought some ideas back home. You may see some similarities to the famous clock's features on the "it's a small world" facade.

Before the ship leaves France, enjoy wine tasting and discover the wine caves in the medieval basements of Cave Historique des Hospices.

In Germany, among the *wunderbar* excursions, visit Heidelberg Castle. Built in 1614, this home of royalty is considered an important Renaissance structure. Sail the Rhine Gorge past 30 other historic castles and a UNESCO World Heritage site.

The last stop is Amsterdam. Highlights include the Rijksmuseum, dedicated to Dutch arts and history; the Rembrandt House Museum, where the painter lived and worked from 1639 to 1656; and the Van Gogh Museum, which boasts more than 1,000 paintings, drawings, and letters by the iconic artist. See the 800-year-old city on a canal cruise. ■

OUT OF THIS WORLD

Welcome to Pandora—The World of Avatar

The Na'vi welcome you to the land inspired by James Cameron's *Avatar* (2009). Walking into Pandora—The World of Avatar is not as simple as walking into the world of a movie (like Cars Land at Disney California Adventure, page 62). Rather, it is an extension of that world. Pandora—The World of Avatar is set on a moon 4.37 light-years from Earth and a generation after the events of the 2009 film "It's your opportunity to go into the planet where all of this occurred, to places that are both familiar and new, and have your own adventure that is yours to own for the day," explains former Imagineer Joe Rohde.

On Pandora, ecotourists have the opportunity to join Alpha Centauri Expeditions (ACE) for the transformational experience of a lifetime. Witness how important nature is to the Na'vi and how much they value conservation. Discover the Valley of Mo'ara with its giant floating mountains and Na'vi drum circle. By day, guests are surrounded by the Pandoran landscape with interactive flora, waterfalls, and flowing streams. At night, the land almost reinvents itself, becoming a bioluminescent forest. Don't just look at the Na'vi culture—listen. It sounds alien. You're in Na'vi territory, after all. You may not see them, but you can hear them.

The ecosystem and its recovery are paramount. "Clearly we know from the film that Pandora has been negatively influenced by this huge mining company and irresponsible mining practices," explains Joe. "And [in the park] you can see how that has impact on the environment. There is a water purification project going on to try to reclean the water and make sure

DEFYING GRAVITY

The floating mountains are one of the most stunning visuals in Pandora—The World of Avatar. The islands of rock are also known as the Hallelujah Mountains and are home to several tribes of Na'vi and banshees. The unobtanium within and beneath them creates a repelling effect, causing them to float. (For further scientific study, see the Meissner effect.) How the Imagineers re-created them in the land is part of the magic.

OPPOSITE: The floating mountains glow with bioluminescence.

PAGES 204-5: Escape to Pandora, the land inspired by James Cameron's *Avatar* (2009).

impurities are removed. There is research into the native species to make sure the normal distribution of the animals that live in this area is restored."

Let's not forget this is Walt Disney World: The attractions and dining are immersive, too. Sail down a mystical river to encounter a Na'vi shaman in Na'vi River Journey. Soar over Pandora on the back of a mountain banshee on Avatar Flight of Passage. Satu'li Canteen supplies travelers with all the comforts of home. Guests may be immersed in an alien moon, but the food is familiar—bowls of wholesome grains, fresh vegetables, and hearty proteins sourced from Pandora's natural abundance. Ready to take a break from exploring? Head over to Pongu Pongu, meaning "Party Party" in the language of the Na'vi. Legend has it that the expat who runs the refreshment stand fell in love with the planet and never left.

"Wherever our guests do come across biological information, ecological information, scientific information in the world of Pandora, we want to make sure that information is based on something real, so they walk away from Pandora with information they can apply to the real world of Earth," concludes Joe. ∎

TUNE IN

Hexapedes (from the Greek *exi*, meaning "six," and the Latin *pedis,* meaning "foot") are six-legged docile creatures. Resembling a cross between a dragon and a gazelle—only blue—they are land herbivores, and a food source for the Na'vi. Because they are hunted, you may not see them when walking through the Valley of Mo'ara, but pay attention—you might spot them along the Kapsavan River on Na'vi River Journey.

PANDORA COME TO LIFE

The Guide to the Flora and Fauna of the Valley of Mo'ara (download from the Experiences tab on *avatar.com*) explains: "Thanks to our partnership with the indigenous Na'vi people, Alpha Centauri Expeditions welcomes you to Pandora—The World of Avatar. A world similar to Earth but unique in so many ways. We encourage you to explore and discover!" With more than 30 species identified in the guide, searching for them is an adventure in itself. When you return to Earth, let the Pandoran flora and fauna continue to inspire you: Care for nature in your own backyard and learn how you can help your favorite animals or plants in the wild.

A: Be transported to another world in Pandora—The World of Avatar. B: A retired walking machine used by the Resources Development Administration, which was behind the irresponsible mining practices on Pandora, stands at the entrance of Pongu Pongu, a great spot for out-of-this-world drinks. C: Fully immerse yourself in Na'vi culture. D: On a visit to Pandora—The World of Avatar, cruise down the Kapsavan River and take in the colorful bioluminescence. E: Take in the otherworldly sights on Na'vi River Journey, which glides down a mysterious river among an extraordinary dreamscape. F. Face painting affords the chance to fully transform and immerse yourself in the world of *Avatar* (2009). G: The menu at Pongu Pongu is inspired by Pandora's natural abundance and includes international and vegetarian cuisine. H: You'll forget you're on planet Earth when you see the larger-than-life wilderness of Pandora.

A

D

SURVIVAL OF THE HAPPIEST

Join the Experts on a Voyage to the Galápagos

Ecuador's Galápagos Islands are a chain of islands, or archipelago, in the eastern Pacific Ocean. There is an abundance of wildlife here; many animal species are endemic, which means they are not found anywhere else in the world. Giant Galápagos tortoises, marine iguanas, Galápagos penguins, and flightless cormorants are found here. Isolated from the mainland for millions of years, it is a rare wilderness sanctuary where animals have no instinctive fear of humans. The islands were made famous by Charles Darwin, who explored the land and observed its creatures, resulting in his theory of evolution.

Scientists have studied the unique ecosystem for more than 180 years. Now it's your turn to examine what makes the destination—also known as Darwin's living laboratory—so special. And National Geographic invites you on an expedition to the Galápagos to do just that. Note that this is an expedition, not a cruise in the traditional sense. Rather than a locked itinerary, the schedule is kept flexible to take advantage of the unexpected and adapt to the opportunities and conditions that arise.

The Lindblad ship is a different style than a typical cruise liner, too. More compact, it provides an inviting home base with comfortable cabins, vibrant public spaces, and dining rooms serving regional cuisine prepared with local ingredients. The expansive decks are designed to be a respite as much as an observation platform. Young travelers are invited to participate in the

OPPOSITE: The giant Galápagos tortoise can weigh up to 920 pounds (417 kg).

PAGES 210-11: From the *National Geographic Endeavour II*, you'll tour the islands and robust natural landscape of the Galápagos.

National Geographic Global Explorers program aboard the ship. Developed with National Geographic Education, this hands-on, interactive program teaches kids how to develop the attitude, skills, and knowledge of an explorer.

The expedition travels between Baltra and San Cristóbal and includes Santa Cruz and a selection of the other islands. Each day, guests have the option to go on nature walks with local naturalists, swim, snorkel, or explore the waters by kayak, glass-bottom boat, or Zodiac.

Ports of call planned on this adventure include Isla Bartolomé, where you'll hike to Bartolomé's volcanic cone for a stunning view of Pinnacle Rock, an imposing spearheaded obelisk rising from the water, before you swim or snorkel with multicolored reef fish and possibly Galápagos penguins. Visit the Charles Darwin Research Station on Santa Cruz, home to several endemic species of giant tortoise, and photograph some of them in the wild. Explore the largest island in the group, Isla Isabela, and look for the only species of flightless cormorant in the world and the only penguin

FUN FACTS

The Galápagos Archipelago is one the most volcanically active areas in the world. The first recorded visitor to the Galápagos was Tomás de Berlanga, whose ship was blown off course in 1535 while sailing from Panama to Peru. An astonishing 97 percent of the Galápagos landmass is designated as a national park. The islands' giant tortoises—after which the archipelago is named—can survive up to one year without food or water.

species that lives this close to the Equator. End the day by snorkeling in the waters that famously attract whales and dolphins.

Isla Floreana offers a chance to spot a flamboyance (yes, that's the term for a group of our pink-feathered friends) of flamingos. The marine iguana haven of Punta Espinoza is located on Isla Fernandina. You'll traverse across hardened lava flows while on the lookout for Galápagos hawks, sea lion nurseries, and—if you missed them before—the rare flightless cormorants. The last island, Española, is a birder's paradise; see swallow-tailed gulls, Española mockingbirds, boobies, and waved albatrosses (seasonally).

End the expedition by spending the day in Guayaquil, a port city known as the "Pearl of the Pacific." Stroll through the narrow cobbled streets of the 400-year-old neighborhood, Las Peñas, and consider climbing the 444 stairs of Santa Ana Hill for panoramic views. ∎

OPPOSITE: The underwater world of the Galápagos Islands—full of endemic species and healthy corals—is just as magnificent as the one on land.

ABOVE: Among its robust species, the islands boast large lizards that don't shy away from humans.

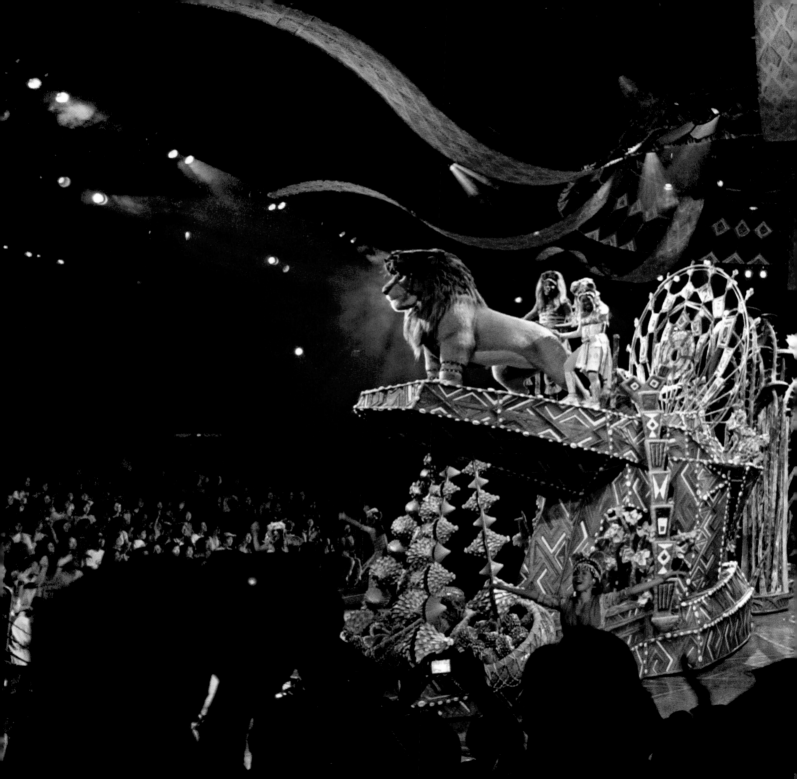

FESTIVAL OF THE LION KING

"Hakuna Matata" is a phrase known in Hong Kong, too. The Circle of Life comes alive on a circular stage as you swing with Timon, Pumbaa, Nala, Scar—and Simba, the Lion King himself. The musical extravaganza debuted at Disney's Animal Kingdom when the park opened in 1998 and became an instant guest favorite. It was soon followed by a version in Hong Kong Disneyland. The show features aerial performances, fire dancers, acrobats, and stunning special effects. You just can't wait to see the Lion King!

IN A GALAXY NOT SO FAR AWAY

Experience *Star Wars: Galactic Starcruiser*

This is the most immersive experience ever created by Disney. The two-day and two-night immersive adventure takes you to a galaxy far, far away.

Once you board the Halcyon starcruiser, you become the star in your own story, creating your persona, making decisions, and choosing alliances. Will you join the Resistance, strike deals with smugglers, or defend the First Order?

Throughout your voyage, characters you've come to know in the *Star Wars* movies are on the ship with you. Meet heroes of the Resistance such as Rey and Chewbacca. Encounter the malevolent Kylo Ren of the First Order. There are new characters joining the adventure, too. Captain Riyola Keevan, Cruise Director Lenka Mok, and astromech droid SK-62O, Mok's devoted assistant. You'll also meet Sammie the Mechanic, and be on the lookout for the intimidating First Order Lt. Harman Croy; he's rumored to be aboard the ship, too. Will you join his team?

Are you eager to be schooled in the ancient ways of wielding a lightsaber? Ready to explore the bridge and learn how it functions from the crew? Hint: This hands-on training may be useful during your voyage. Because this is a vacation, perhaps you prefer to savor a cocktail at the Sublight Lounge or dine in the Crown of Corellia Dining Room. Whatever you choose, the fate of the galaxy is in your hands. ∎

Star Wars: Galactic Starcruiser is a two-night immersive experience.

A PRIVATE OASIS

Sunbathe on the Shores of Disney's Very Own Bahamian Island

It used to be a far-flung notion that an average person could visit a private island. Disney Cruise Line changed all that in 1998. Castaway Cay is reserved exclusively for Disney Cruise Line guests on its Bahamian and Caribbean cruises. (Tip: Although it's accepted, *cay* does not rhyme with *way*. It's pronounced like *key*.) Only one ship docks there at a time, allowing for uncrowded beaches and plenty of room for fun in the sun.

Snorkel in the clear blue lagoon; beginners can follow the Discover Trail, while the Explorer Trail beckons the more experienced. Be sure to keep your dive masks sparkling to spot the Hidden Mickey (page 136). Swim to Pelican Plunge, a giant floating water play platform with two twisting waterslides. Fans of floating can rent kayaks, paddleboats, aqua trikes, inner tubes, and stand-up paddleboards. For a break from the sun, visit the In Da Shade Game Pavilion, which offers table tennis, billiards, foosball, and basketball. Adults can escape to secluded Serenity Bay, where you can book an open-air cabana massage and enjoy refreshing frozen cocktails. In turn, teens have their own hideout, too.

The airstrip is the setting for the Castaway Cay 5K. Guests can run, jog, or walk along the scenic shores and past the observation tower. After crossing the finish line, you're rewarded with an exclusive Castaway Cay 5K medal. Add it to your collection of *run*Disney event medals (page 118).

There will be smiles for miles when you reboard the ship for your next Disney adventure! ∎

Goofy, Donald Duck, and friends join guests on the shores of Castaway Cay.

CONSERVATION STATION

Get Involved in Rafiki's Planet Watch

Tucked in the rear of the Africa area of Disney's Animal Kingdom, and named for the mandrill and sage shaman of *The Lion King* (1994), Rafiki's Planet Watch is a multifaceted, interactive, and educational attraction not to be missed. The sign above the entrance encourages guests to "Open Your Eyes and See the World." But first, you'll need to walk the short distance though the verdant forest to Harambe Station. There you'll board the Wildlife Express Train for a backstage journey behind Disney's Animal Kingdom. The behind-the-scenes sights along the way include the perimeter of Kilimanjaro Safaris, rhino barns, and Tembo House, where the elephants are kept at night.

After disembarking, you'll pass education kiosks on your way to **Conservation Station.** You can learn lots in this building, beginning with the expert veterinary care all the park's animals receive. The treatment room is on full display behind a large glass window. Observe procedures—usually after the first train arrives—an amazing opportunity for your budding vet! Nearby is the Animal Nutrition Center, where the team prepares more than 1,000 specialized diets daily for the park's 3,000-plus mammals, birds, reptiles, and fish. They use the same high-quality fruits and vegetables that are served to guests in Disney restaurants.

The Animation Experience at Conservation Station is an homage to Walt and his practice of encouraging his animators to spend time around

IMAGINE THIS

"The story of Disney's Animal Kingdom and the Disney Conservation Fund is not just a story we tell. It's a story we are living every day," says former Imagineer Joe Rohde. "We've worked toward a dream: a dream of a future for our children in which there is still magic in the forest, the magic that comes from the countless miraculous creatures . . . that share with us a tiny delicate place amidst a sea of distant stars."

OPPOSITE: The vets at Rafiki's Planet Watch care for animals across Walt Disney World.

PAGES 222-3: Rafiki guides you through animal facts in Rafiki's Planet Watch.

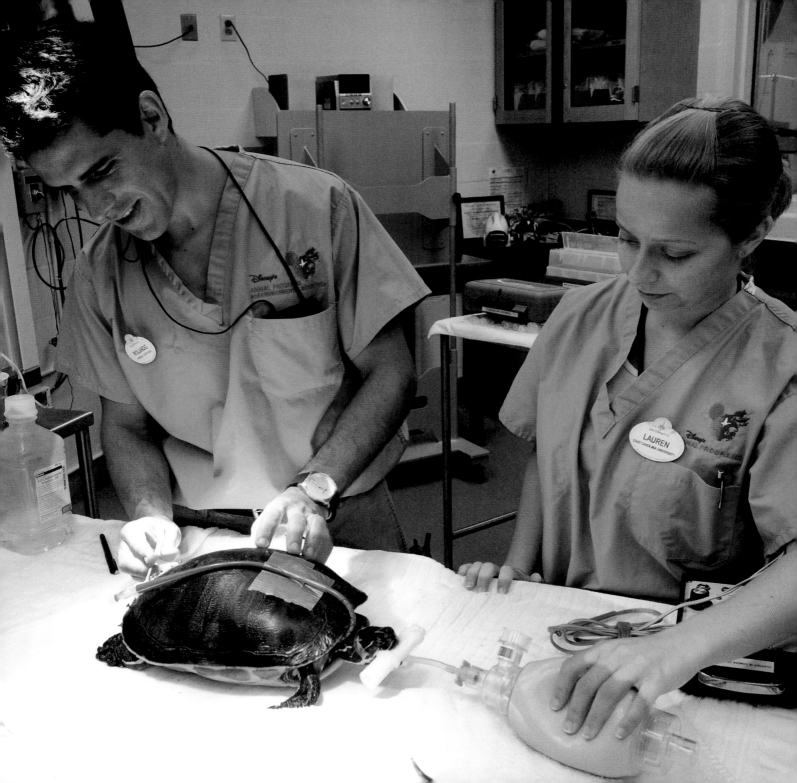

WHO ARE THE PEOPLE CARING FOR COTTON-TOP TAMARINS?

SCIENTISTS study wild cotton-tops to learn about their role in the forest ecosystem.

LOCAL PEOPLE in learn to appreciate cotton-tops and ho share the forest's with them.

CONSERVATIONISTS use cotton-tops as ambassadors to help spread awareness.

PEOPLE LIK supporting above and b fore

animals to appreciate their forms and learn from their unique behaviors. For instance, when *Bambi* (1942) was being made, deer were brought to the studio as inspiration. Today, participants in these 25-minute classes receive step-by-step instruction on how to illustrate their own versions of popular Disney characters.

Recognizing that park guests love to celebrate animals, **Affection Section** offers opportunities for guests to meet and touch them up close and personal. All the domesticated creatures—including goats, sheep, and pigs—have a choice to interact or not in the thoughtfully designed outdoor space. For the latter, animals are trained to recognize an area encircled by a blue rope as "safe" from human interaction. This is a kind and gentle experience for guests—and animals—of all ages.

As you conclude your time at Conservation Station, remember Mufasa's wise words to Simba in *The Lion King:* "Everything you see exists together in a delicate balance. As king, you need to understand that balance and respect all the creatures, from the crawling ant to the leaping antelope." ∎

MORE FROM WALT

"Conservation isn't just the business of a few people," Walt Disney once said, "it's a matter that concerns all of us. It's a science whose principles are written in the oldest code in the world—the laws of nature. The natural resources of our vast continent are not inexhaustible, but if we will use our riches wisely, if we will protect our wildlife and preserve our lakes and streams, these things will last us for generations to come."

EXPLAINED IN BLACK AND WHITE

A

The Walt Disney Company is passionately committed to the protection of rhinos and the natural habitats they need to survive and thrive. Large-scale poaching caused a near-total collapse in black rhino populations between 1960 and 1995, and current demand for rhino horns is causing a staggering increase in poaching. The white rhino population in Uganda has been extinct since 1982. In 2006, two white rhinos, both born at Disney's Animal Kingdom, traveled from Florida to Africa in the first ever reintroduction of white rhinos from the United States to Uganda. How can you help? Never buy anything made from rhino horns.

A: The Disney Conservation Fund helped the Dian Fossey Gorilla Fund International open the Gorilla Rehabilitation and Conservation Education (GRACE) Center in the Democratic Republic of the Congo. B: Exhibits throughout Conservation Station in Disney's Animal Kingdom highlight conservation efforts around the world. C: Rafiki welcomes you to explore a menagerie of animal activities at Conservation Station. D: Cross the African savanna on the Wildlife Express Train for a behind-the-scenes look at Disney's Animal Kingdom. E: Encounter adorable animals at Affection Section in Disney's Animal Kingdom. F: Experts and educators share how they care for the animals at Affection Section. G: Three white rhinos were born in Disney's Animal Kingdom between 2020 and 2021. H: Manatees are cared for at The Seas with Nemo & Friends pavilion at EPCOT with the goal of returning them to the wild.

D

B

C

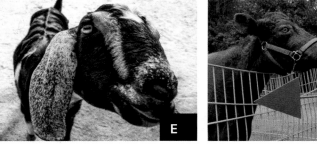

E

F

G

H

THE ARTIST'S MUSE

Escape to Copenhagen, Denmark, on a Walt-Inspired Tour

The Adventures by Disney Copenhagen Escape is a four-day whirlwind of Danish—and Disney—history. Take it on its own or add the tour to a Disney Cruise Line vacation.

The story begins with Walt's travels to Europe. On each European trip (he took more than 20 in his lifetime), he'd visit zoos, fairs, circuses, and carnivals, all of which inspired pieces of his own amusement park. Unfortunately, he found almost all of them dirty and disappointing. However, on a trip to Denmark in 1951, he made a discovery. Walt's biographer Bob Thomas describes the scene in *Walt Disney: An American Original:* "His spirit revived when he saw Tivoli Gardens in Copenhagen; it was spotless and brightly colored and priced within the reach of everyone. The gaiety of the music, the excellence of the food and drink, the warm courtesy of the employees—everything combined for a pleasurable experience. 'Now *this* is what an amusement park is supposed to be!' Walt enthused."

When you arrive in Denmark's capital city, you'll have the day to explore on your own. Here you can discover why Danes are considered among the happiest people on the planet, delve into famed Danish design, and treat yourself to one of the world's most innovative cuisines.

Later comes your opportunity to see what impressed Walt so much. Tivoli Gardens is among the oldest amusement parks in the world. Its whimsical architecture and lush gardens are legendary. The multitude of exciting attractions range from the modern, such as the Aquila with the centrifugal force of 4 g, to one of the oldest functioning wooden roller coasters still operating today; it was originally built in 1914. Just like Walt was with Disneyland, Tivoli

ON A ROLL

About 350 years ago in France, an apprentice baker from Austria made a big goof: He forgot to add the butter to the flour. Attempting to fix his error, he added lumps of butter to his already mixed dough. The result was not a disaster. It was a triumph! From there the pastry migrated to Denmark. Danes call it "Viennese" because of Austria's role in the pastry's history. Germans call it "Copenhagener." Americans refer to it simply as "Danish."

OPPOSITE: In Copenhagen, visit Frederiksborg Castle, built for King Christian IV in the early 17th century.

PAGES 228-9: Gilded frescoes adorn the ceilings and walls inside Frederiksborg Castle.

Gardens is dedicated to constant improvement and innovation; it maintains its historic feel with a foot firmly in the 21st century. As is the case with all Disney theme parks, the food is a big part of the fun here. Choose from more than 35 restaurants for lunch and dinner. For fans of Disneyland, this is considered a pilgrimage.

Spend a day with Hans Christian Andersen, one of Denmark's most famous citizens and a national treasure. He wrote several familiar fairy tales (many of which inspired Disney animated films), including "The Ugly Duckling," "The Princess and the Pea," "Thumbelina," "The Emperor's New Clothes," and "The Little Mermaid," which was turned into an instant Disney classic in 1989. A statue dedicated to Andersen's "The Little Mermaid" is one of Copenhagen's most popular attractions. Visit the landmark, take photos, and share the history behind the under-the-sea adventure with your kids.

Then it's on to the Viking Ship Museum in Roskilde. Tour the collection of Viking ships dating back to the 11th century and learn how boats

THE A-LIST

Hans Christian Andersen's "The Little Mermaid," written in Copenhagen, was published in 1837. It became the Disney animated classic by the same name more than 150 years later. Ariel, the heroine in the Disney film, is the youngest of King Triton's seven daughters. Can you name her sisters? Hint: They all start with A just like Ariel: Aquata, Andrina, Arista, Attina, Adella, and Alana.

are being made today using centuries-old methods. King Christian IV built Frederiksborg Castle in the early 17th century. Tour the grounds before heading to Kronborg, Denmark's most famous castle. Kronborg, also known as "Elsinore" thanks to William Shakespeare's naming of the castle in *Hamlet,* was constructed around 1420. Here you're treated to a privately guided tour to learn about the major roles the castle has played in history. The farewell dinner is held at Tivolihallen, a highly regarded eatery included in the book *1,001 Restaurants You Must Experience Before You Die.*

On the final day, enjoy a Scandinavian tradition: *fika.* An aspect of Swedish culture that has taken hold in Denmark, fika is a time when people come together to enjoy coffee, companionship, and a bite to eat. After this Copenhagen pilgrimage, you'll likely repeat Ariel's proclamation: "Have you ever seen anything so wonderful in your entire life?" ∎

THE MERRY-GO-ROUND IN GRIFFITH PARK

Griffith Park in Los Angeles has been the home to the iconic merry-go-round since 1937. Built in 1926 by the Spillman Engineering Company, it features 68 horses, all of them finely carved jumpers with jewel-encrusted bridles. It also boasts a Stinson 165 Military Band Organ that plays more than 1,500 selections of marches and waltzes. What's notable about this location is its remarkable connection to Walt Disney and Disneyland: "[The idea for Disneyland] came about when my daughters were very young and Saturday was always daddy's day with the two daughters," said Walt. "So we'd start out and try to go someplace, you know, different things, and I'd take them to the merry-go-round . . . and as I'd sit while they rode the merry-go-round . . . sit on a bench, you know, eating peanuts—I felt there should be something built where the parents and the children could have fun together. So that's how Disneyland started."

When Walt's great American theme park was being designed, one of the planned Opening Day attractions was King Arthur Carrousel in Fantasyland. He purchased a 1922 Dentzel carousel from a Toronto amusement park, supplementing it with Murphy horses from a Coney Island carousel. As he wanted only jumping horses—just like his merry-go-round inspiration in Griffith Park—the standers, or stationary ones, were retrofitted to go up and down. The assorted other animals were put in storage and the carriages were removed and repurposed as cars for Casey Jr. Circus Train.

OPPOSITE: Take your turn on the iconic Griffith Park Merry-Go-Round, built in 1926.

PAGES 234–5: Walt took this photo of his daughters, Diane (left) and Sharon (right), on a "daddy's day."

In total, King Arthur Carrousel at Disneyland has 68 horses, 17 rows of four abreast, and one bench for guests using wheelchairs. The lead horse is named Jingles; it was rededicated to honor Julie Andrews in 2008.

The Griffith Park Merry-Go-Round is a treasure not just for Los Angeles but for the world. It's also one of the last historic merry-go-rounds operating in America and a fun way to connect with Walt outside of Disneyland. Bring some peanuts, sit on a bench, and go for a spin or two. The landmark attraction is open only on the weekends. If you plan your trip for the third Sunday of the month, consider adding Walt's Barn (page 128) to your itinerary as it's very close by. ∎

MORE FROM WALT

Way back in 1939, Walt apprised studio staffers (and brothers) Bill and Bob Jones about his confidential—and still far-off—park project that would eventually evolve into Disneyland. Bob recalled Walt's instructions: "Besides a merry-go-round, there could be other rides, but they should all be safe and attractive." It was Bob's impression that Walt considered the merry-go-round a priority for attraction options.

AMERICA'S BEST IDEA

Adventure With Experts to Two Iconic National Parks

The great American West beckons you on this journey to two of America's national treasures: Yellowstone and Grand Teton National Parks.

On arrival in Bozeman, Montana, attend an after-hours visit to the Museum of the Rockies. You'll see "Dinosaurs Under the Big Sky" at the Siebel Dinosaur Complex, one of the largest and most up-to-date dinosaur exhibits in the world. In the museum, you'll also find one of the few mounted *Tyrannosaurus rex* skeletons in the United States as well as the bones of Big Al, a nearly complete *Allosaurus* that lived during the Jurassic period.

The adventure continues in Yellowstone National Park. Established by Congress in 1872 as a "public park and pleasuring-ground for the benefit and enjoyment of the people," it was the world's first designated national park. Have lunch in the shadows of the Absaroka mountain range and spend the day exploring the steaming travertine terraces of Mammoth Hot Springs. Then visit the wildlife-rich Lamar Valley, in the northern part of the park. This is where gray wolves were first restored to Yellowstone in 1995. Meet a renowned wildlife photographer in his home studio and learn about his experiences capturing images for *National Geographic* magazine.

Then you're off to the other Grand Canyon—the one located in Yellowstone—where two staggered falls spill water from twice the height of the famous Niagara Falls. Be on the lookout for bison, coyotes, elk, and perhaps an awe-inspiring grizzly bear in Hayden Valley. Across the Continental Divide you'll make your way into the Upper Geyser Basin, home of the famed Old Faithful Geyser, which got its name because of its reliable eruption schedule.

OPPOSITE: Yellowstone's Grand Prismatic Spring, made colorful by microbes in the water and silt, is the largest hot spring in the United States.

PAGES 238-9: See the abundant buffalo that roam the plains of Yellowstone National Park.

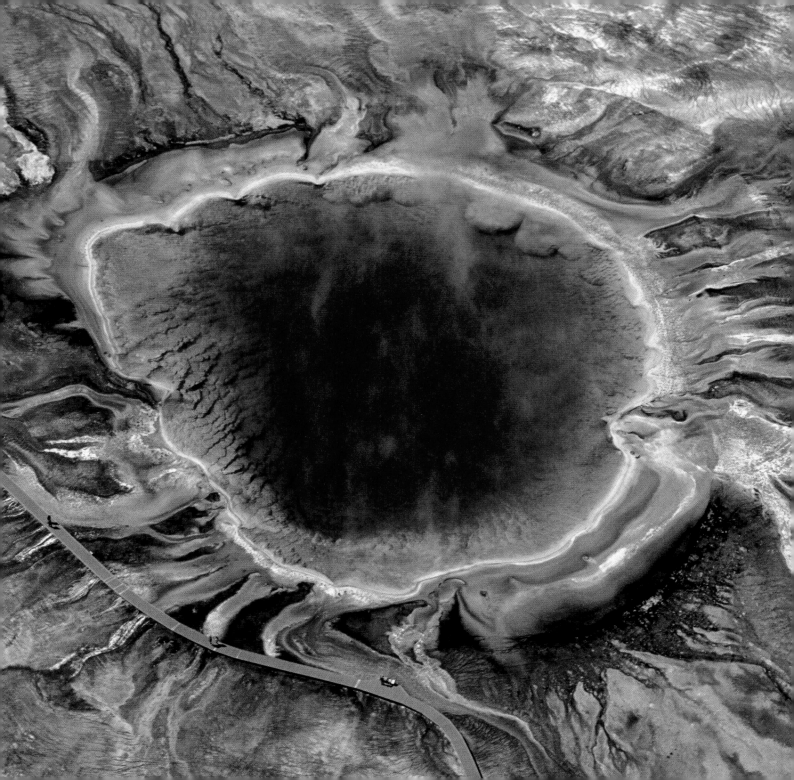

Continue your adventure in Upper Geyser Basin by learning about the geothermal landscape, including Yellowstone's geysers, which account for two-thirds of all those found throughout the world. At night, a National Geographic expert will give a fascinating lecture preparing you for Wyoming's Grand Teton National Park.

The itinerary in Grand Teton features the Craig Thomas Discovery and Visitor Center. Enjoy modern exhibits about preservation and mountaineering, plus view a selection of Native American artifacts in the David T. Vernon Collection. Then continue to the historic Murie Ranch, where the 1964 Wilderness Act was born. A private presentation will explain the history of this location and its importance in ushering in the modern conservationist movement.

Before you say goodbye to the grandeur of these parks, join a tour of the National Museum of Wildlife Art in Jackson, Wyoming. Finish with a float down the Snake River as you keep your eyes peeled for a variety of wildlife and woodland creatures. ■

MORE FROM WALT

A fan of winter sports, Walt enjoyed Yosemite National Park. There, he met Austrian ski champion and instructor Hannes Schroll. Walt later invested in Hannes's nearby Sugar Bowl Resort. Honoring Walt, Hannes renamed one of the peaks "Mount Disney," and it remains open today. The first chairlift in California (1939) is named for Disney, too, as are the runs Disney Meadow, Disney Traverse, Disney Nose, and the Donald Duck. Sugar Bowl is also the setting for 1941's *The Art of Skiing* starring Goofy.

VOYAGEURS' LOUNGE

W alt once said: "There is more treasure in books than in all the pirates' loot on Treasure Island . . ."

This cozy library-inspired setting, tucked away off the lobby of Disney's Riviera Resort in Walt Disney World, is a treasure trove. The volumes (not available for reading; they are affixed on the shelves) highlight Walt's world adventures and the types of books he collected during his trip to Europe in 1935; many later inspired the movies and attractions we love today.

Browse the titles and memorabilia on the shelves. The items and reproductions offer a glimpse into Walt's travels, inspired by original and similar historic artifacts preserved in the Walt Disney Archives and at The Walt Disney Family Museum. Relax and stay a while: Coffee, tea, light bites, pastries, and cocktails are available from the adjacent Le Petit Café.

LET US GO

Inspired by Elsa and Anna, This Norwegian Adventure Packs in All the Fun

When Elsa and Anna were introduced to the world with *Frozen* in 2013, Norway may not have been on a lot of Disney fans' radars. Thanks to the popularity of the film, however, and its Scandinavian-inspired fictional kingdom, Arendelle, it is now at the top of many families' lists. Fulfill your fantasy by joining Adventures by Disney for an eight-day vacation to the snowcapped mountains, fjords, and glacial lakes of Norway and the Scandinavian Peninsula.

Your adventure begins in the town of Bergen, whose old-world charm was one of the filmmakers' inspirations for Arendelle. Accommodations are in the historic Bryggen area, the first of several UNESCO World Heritage sites on your Nordic journey. Then it's off to the "adventure capital of Norway," Voss, where you'll glide with your family on a river raft past the region's majestic mountains.

The tour also brings you to Flåm, where you'll find out that safaris aren't just for jeeps and Africa. Enjoy a safari of a different kind: a boat adventure with cultural sightseeing. Riding a rigid inflatable boat (RIB), you'll explore the nooks and crannies of the fjord. Discover villages along the way, and listen to the lore of local storytellers. Visit Nærøyfjord, a UNESCO World Heritage site, and see an ancient Viking burial ground.

When you arrive in Laerdal, you're treated to something you may recognize from *Frozen*, the Borgund Stave Church. Stave churches (a medieval wooden church with four central upright logs and vertical planks for walls) are iconic structures in Norway and provided architectural inspiration for the film. (Visit the Stave Church Gallery in World Showcase at EPCOT before

OPPOSITE: **Borgund Stave Church, built in 1180, is one of the most well-preserved medieval wooden churches of a type common in northwestern Europe at the time of its construction.**

PAGES 244-5: **The fjords of Norway offer breathtaking beauty around every bend.**

or after your trip to learn more.) Stand in awe in Geirangerfjord, a UNESCO World Heritage site and home to stunning scenery and the Seven Sisters waterfall, which plummets a remarkable 1,345 feet (410 m). Dinner that evening is for adults and camaraderie. Junior Adventurers will dine in the hotel's "car garage," which showcases car-related treasures. Afterward, it's time for a karaoke sing-along and an activity making—what else?—trolls!

Westerås Farm is next on the agenda. Wander the hills and learn about local life. Meet a Norwegian family and greet their farm animals. Perhaps you'll spot a reindeer, one just like Sven, the "funny-looking donkey" and Kristoff's loyal sidekick. From there, hike to the hills to see Storseterfossen waterfall (weather permitting). The popular trail leads to a stunning view of the waterfall that shares a feature with Schweitzer Falls from the Jungle Cruise at Disneyland—it's seen from behind! The crystal clear water of Lake Loen is the perfect setting for net fishing the following morning. That

ICEBREAKER

The dynamic opening scene in *Frozen* (2013) shows the ice cutters—and little Kristoff with young Sven—harvesting frozen water. The tradition in Norway began back when there were no refrigerators. The practice still exists today, though chain saws tend to replace hand axes. Just as in the film, the ice is sawed into even-sized blocks and hauled away from the lake. How are they used in modern times? Among other purposes, they're used for ice sculptures, high-end cocktails, and ice hotels.

afternoon, bike 45 minutes to a nearby glacier, Kjenndalsbreen. Head to your retreat at the Hotel Union. Car buffs will want to see the collection of automobiles that were used to show tourists around the village of Geiranger in the 1920s and '30s. Chauffeurs are available if you want to take a spin. Dinner is a Norwegian-style barbecue in the hotel's traditional grass-roofed cabin.

Just like your favorite movie, all good things must come to an end. And this trip ends in Oslo, Norway's capital city. Travel by train through the scenic countryside to reach your final destination. The farewell dinner is held in a private room in the famed Grand Hotel Oslo; you and your fellow adventurers will be entertained by traditional folk dancers. After a restful sleep and a hearty breakfast, transfer to the airport and board your flight home. But not before saying *farvel*—or goodbye—to *Frozen* land. ∎

OPPOSITE: Set off on a fjord safari: Ride a rigid inflatable boat (RIB) into the nooks and crannies of Aurlandsfjord and Nærøyfjord.

ABOVE: Marvel at the greenery and peaks at stopping points and restaurants along your tour throughout Norway.

FOR THE FIRST TIME IN FOREVER

I f there ever was an anthem for a Disney feature, "Let It Go" from *Frozen* (2013) may be it. The showstopper was written by husband-and-wife songwriting team Kristen Anderson-Lopez and Robert Lopez. Intended to convey Elsa's exhilaration about letting go of all she was holding on to inside, the song was written in just a day and a half! It won the Academy Award for Best Original Song in 2014.

Now to celebrate the fan-favorite film and its winterful tunes, a *Frozen*-themed land is coming to a Disney park! The Kingdom of Arendelle at Disneyland Paris will feature Elsa's Ice Castle perched on a 131-foot (40-m) snow-covered mountain, a village reminiscent of the one in the film, a Nordic-inspired restaurant, plus a brand-new attraction. In summer or any other season, Olaf and the gang will welcome guests and ensure an experience worth melting for.

CRUISE WITH THE STARS

A Members-Only Experience at Sea

There are thousands of unique offerings for Disney Vacation Club members, but there is typically only *one* Member Cruise a year—and it is, indeed, memorable!

All Disney cruises are magical; however, this one is in a class all by itself. And it's first class all the way. From the moment you embark, the atmosphere is abuzz with anticipation. Although the coveted itinerary is announced months in advance, the surprises to come are not. As the ship pulls away from the dock, the fanfare of the Sail Away Party begins. Mickey and friends get the celebration started, and just when you think it can't possibly get any more exciting, it does. It's time to meet the Disney Vacation Club Member Cruise's celebrity guests. They change from year to year, cruise to cruise, with past superstars including Pete Docter, director of Pixar favorites *Monsters, Inc.* (2001), *Up* (2009), *Inside Out* (2015), and *Soul* (2020); Auli'i Cravalho, the voice of Moana; Disney Legend and Imagineer Tony Baxter, creator of the iconic Big Thunder Mountain Railroad, Indiana Jones Adventure, and Splash Mountain attractions; Broadway star Ashley Brown of *Mary Poppins* fame; *Beauty and the Beast* and *The Lion King* producer Don Hahn; the people behind the voices of Goofy (Disney Legend Bill Farmer) and Mickey Mouse (Bret Iwan); stage and screen star Jennifer Hudson; and Disney Legend Floyd Norman, an animator who began working with Walt in the 1950s. With such diversity represented in the lineup, there's

LEGEND HAS IT

We have architect and Disney Legend Wing T. Chao to thank for the first two Disney cruise ships. Wing led the design of the *Magic* and *Wonder,* as well as later ships such as the *Dream* and *Fantasy.*

OPPOSITE: From left to right: Bret Iwan (voice of Mickey Mouse), Disney Legend Bill Farmer (voice of Goofy), and Pixar veteran Bob Peterson (voice of Roz from 2001's *Monsters, Inc.* and Dug from 2009's *Up*) have been featured on board.

PAGES 252-3: No detail is spared aboard the ship.

sure to be something, and someone, to delight every Disney fan.

These are not hands-off experiences. You'll have the opportunity to interact with these remarkable guests during panel presentations, seminars, meet and greets, and drawing lessons, and you'll also get behind-the-scenes and sneak peeks of upcoming Disney films.

A signature for this special sailing are the gifts delivered to your stateroom while you're away. That's every day, twice a day. Repeat Disney Vacation Club Member Cruise passengers know to pack an empty suitcase or duffel bag for all the swag, which on past voyages has included such favorites as logoed glasses, custom beach towels, and portable Bluetooth speakers to play all your favorite Disney music.

Additional perks may include nighttime cabarets hosted by Disney recording artists, themed deck parties, specialty menu and cocktail items, Broadway-style productions, and special exhibits curated by the Walt Disney Archives. ∎

MINNIE HAS A MESSAGE FOR YOU

You've booked your Disney cruise. Now the countdown begins. Get the entire family excited with Character Calls, complimentary prerecorded calls from select Disney characters. (Arrange the call time online under My Disney Cruise.) Minnie (or others) will call to wish you a magical voyage. (Note: You're limited to two calls per reservation.)

TWO FOR ONE

One Vacation. Two Disney Parks. Thousands of Years of History.

Talk about bang for your buck: On this one-of-a-kind tour from Adventures by Disney, you'll marvel at the traditions, natural wonders, and vibrant history of China on a 12-day excursion across six cities.

The trip begins in Hong Kong, where you'll have a chance to acclimate yourself at the Peninsula Hong Kong hotel, opened in 1928 and known as the "Grand Dame of the Far East." Experience Hong Kong Disneyland and its seven magical lands. Pay special attention to the historic and newly reimagined Castle of Magical Dreams. Inspired by dreamers and believers, it stands proudly as the centerpiece of the theme park and as a symbol of hope and possibility.

Next, you're off to Beijing for two full days of sightseeing. You'll see the Temple of Heaven, which UNESCO deems a "masterpiece of architecture and landscape design." Tour the Forbidden City and its 90 palaces, including courtyards, 10,000-plus rooms, grand halls, courts, and banquet rooms. Travel by pedicab through the narrow streets, or *hutongs,* of the city's ancient neighborhoods. Last, but certainly not least, walk along one of the new wonders of the world—the Great Wall of China!

Fly to Xi'an to explore a UNESCO World Cultural Heritage site, the Mausoleum of the First Qin Emperor, with its terracotta warriors. The more than 7,000 clay sculptures of warriors, horses, and chariots were found buried alongside unified China's first emperor, Qin Shi Huang, during an archaeological dig in 1974.

Other highlights may include: a cruise on the Li River with breathtaking

KNOW BEFORE YOU GO

Even though the Seven Dwarfs did it daily, whistling in China is considered rude. Chinese people point with an open hand, never with an index finger. Slurp your soup! It's a sign of appreciation. Tap two fingers twice on the table after being served tea to thank the person pouring it. It's polite to present and receive items with both hands. Don't be like the White Rabbit: Punctuality is considered a virtue.

OPPOSITE: Visit all seven magical lands, including Fantasyland, on the tour's stop at Hong Kong Disneyland.

PAGES 256-7: Along with visiting the parks, see historical landmarks, including the Great Wall of China.

views of the "gumdrop mountains"; traditional tai chi taught by a master; Sichuan opera—a marvel of music, circus-like stunts, puppetry, and the magic of "face changing," where performers change vividly colored masks with lightning speed; and pandas! Enjoy a private tour of the Chengdu Research Base of Giant Panda Breeding, then observe the pandas at play in their natural habitat enclosures.

Shanghai brings a classic Chinese acrobat show, a stroll through the Old City, and contemplative time in the 300-year-old Yu Garden. Conclude your vacation at Shanghai Disneyland. Ride classic attractions and take in some new ones, including those unique to this park, such as Pirates of the Caribbean: Battle for the Sunken Treasure in Treasure Cove (page 138). ∎

HONG KONG HISTORY

Hong Kong Disneyland opened its gates on September 12, 2005, making Disney history as the first Disney theme park to open in China. Debuting with four traditional lands, it now has seven, including Grizzly Gulch and Mystic Point—home to an attraction centered on the eccentric adventurer Lord Henry Mystic.

SPLASHTACULAR!

Soar on a Water Adventure With Mickey and Minnie

When you wish upon a star, your dreams do come true. At least on the brand-new *Disney Wish*. The ship has a few firsts: Captain Minnie adorning the bow and the first ever Disney attraction at sea—the AquaMouse! As with all Disney attractions, there is a story that goes along with the thrill. Port Misadventures is the name of Mickey and Minnie's seaside excursion company, after all. Mickey and Minnie invite you on an undersea journey to Mermaid Lagoon—with plenty of hijinks!

The water ride, with its two-seater vehicles, will send you on an adventure through 760 feet (230 m) of winding tubes. Along the journey you'll ascend into a magical tunnel, encounter a cartoon world featuring brand-new animated shorts that play out through oversize virtual portholes, and see familiar Disney pals. There are special effects galore—all synced to an original musical score by Emmy-nominated composer Christopher Willis. Be on the lookout for Disney Easter eggs. Hiding in each show are Chip and Dale hitch-hiking their way to Castaway Cay, Disney's private island (page 218). The abominable snowman from Disneyland's Matterhorn Bobsleds makes an appearance, too.

Keep your hands and arms inside the aqua vehicle as you dash around the upper decks and through a dark tunnel that ultimately reveals a stunning view of the ocean. After jetting up and down a series of speed blasters and a soaring loop over the edge of the ship, you'll splash down! And you'll no doubt want to rebook with Mickey and Minnie to be a Port Misadventures passenger again. ∎

Aboard the *Disney Wish*, a ride on AquaMouse takes you through two animated shorts: *Scuba Scramble* and *Swiss Meltdown*.

BE OUR GUEST

From Counter Service to
White Tablecloth Dining

Grab a bite at the Sci-Fi Dine-In Theater Restaurant, a 1950s-style diner where retro cars are your table and sci-fi movie clips play during the meal.

DINE LIKE ROYALTY

Enjoy a Regal Feast at Be Our Guest Restaurant and Cinderella's Royal Table

Lumiere advised in *Beauty and the Beast* (1991), "If you're stressed, it's fine dining we suggest."

So why not take a break from the hustle and bustle of the park and be pampered for a spell?

Get the royal treatment at the most magical restaurants in the Magic Kingdom, where Disney's popular movies *Cinderella* (1950) and *Beauty and the Beast* come to life. At these beloved establishments, fine dining and storytelling intersect. Children will be enchanted as they step right into their favorite films—only in 3D!

Located inside Beast's castle in Fantasyland, Be Our Guest Restaurant boasts three themed dining rooms that will transport you back in time. In the grand Ballroom, you'll be swept away by the Gothic grandeur of the chandeliers, the draperies, and the mural on the ceiling, all re-created from the movie. It's also where Beast makes his grand entrance. Beast's private chamber is in the West Wing—not off-limits here. In front of the large arched window is the Enchanted Rose. Watch the nearby portrait as it switches from Prince to Beast when a petal falls. And the final space, the Rose Gallery, boasts a larger-than-life music box with Belle and Beast dancing.

The French-inspired fare is presented in regal fashion for lunch and dinner. Children can create their own three-course meals. When it comes to dessert, Lumiere reminds us, "Try the Grey Stuff, it's delicious. Don't believe me? Ask the dishes!" The Grey Stuff—a tasty creamy concoction—is very popular with Disney foodies; if you've never tasted it, Beast's castle is the perfect place.

SEW AND SEW

Jaq and Gus are the beloved tiny tailors who helped make Cinderella's pink dress for the ball. You may have met their mice counterparts, Suzy and Perla, in the parks. But have you heard of Mert, Bert, Luke, and Blossom? Although they're not individually identified in the film, these mice were mentioned in the studio production notes as characters.

OPPOSITE: A meal at Cinderella's Royal Table includes good food and a chance to meet your favorite princess.

PAGES 264-5: Dine like royalty in Beast's castle at Be Our Guest Restaurant.

"A dream is a wish your heart makes," sang Cinderella, and surely this next experience will be a dream come true.

Cinderella Castle at Walt Disney World was partly inspired by famous French palace-fortresses and châteaus. Disney Legend and chief designer Herb Ryman also referenced the original designs from the 1950 *Cinderella* animated feature. (Tokyo Disneyland has a Cinderella Castle, too; however, it doesn't have a restaurant inside.) Cinderella's Royal Table is the crown jewel restaurant in the Magic Kingdom. Look for the Disney family crest on the fireplace before your royal party is called. The spiral staircase—or gilded elevator—leads to the resplendent dining room. There, in a storybook setting with stained glass windows overlooking Fantasyland, breakfast, lunch, and dinner are served. All meals are prix fixe (fixed price). Cinderella may appear, proving that fairy tales do come true.

Advance reservations (available up to 60 days prior) are highly suggested and require park reservation and admission. ∎

COLORFUL STORYTELLING

The color of Belle's clothing has meaning in *Beauty and the Beast* (1991). In her small 18th-century French village, she is the only character who wears the color blue. As Belle and Beast fall in love, Belle's clothing colors get warmer—such as her pink coat in the "Something There" snow scene; her pale green dress when she's surprised with the library; and her gorgeous yellow gown when dancing with Beast in the grand Ballroom.

TAKE A TRIP TO THE TROPICS

Cheers to Exploration and Adventure

Trader Sam is a legendary explorer. He's also a legendary bartender. He's been known to search Polynesia, the Amazon, Congo, Nile, Mekong, and other exotic locales looking for ingredients for his creative concoctions. When Sam first landed at Disneyland, he established the world-famous Trader Sam's Enchanted Tiki Bar. Buoyed by that success, he set sail east, arriving at the Seven Seas Lagoon and X marked the spot where he would open his next outpost: the Grog Grotto.

Like any adventurer, Sam has collected trinkets and treasures. Maritime mementos festoon the lounges, too. At Trader Sam's Grog Grotto in Disney's Polynesian Village Resort, the Nautilus cocktail is a tribute to fellow adventurer Jules Verne and his novel *20,000 Leagues Under the Sea* (also a beloved former attraction at Walt Disney World). The submarine-shaped glass may be obvious; however, you'll find more to explore. For instance, look for the photo of Walt Disney holding one of the movie's giant squid's eight arms.

Over in Trader Sam's Enchanted Tiki Bar at the Disneyland Hotel, homage is paid to the Jungle Cruise attraction in Adventureland with the HippopotoMai-Tai and Piranha Pool cocktails. Look for the "Easter eggs"—a term for hidden references and inside jokes—throughout the nooks, crannies, and shelves of all of Sam's establishments. Just like cast members in the parks, the bartenders—called skippers—make magic, too. But you'll have to get one of the coveted seats to experience it for yourself. ∎

Trader Sam's Grog Grotto in Disney's Polynesian Village Resort offers tropical drinks and bar fare.

SHARE A MEAL WITH MICKEY AND FRIENDS

Breakfast, Lunch, and Dinner With Your Favorite Characters

"Other people can have their bands, thrill rides, and all this stuff, but we've got the Disney characters, and don't think they aren't important! When you see people come in with their children and one of our characters appears, they run to them and get their cameras," said Walt Disney.

Walt's words still ring true today; however, the idea of combining dining and Disney characters didn't begin until the 1970s at the Snow White in the Village Restaurant at what is now Disney Springs. Minnie's Menehune, which premiered in the late 1970s, was one of the first character breakfasts at Disney's Polynesian Village Resort. Hostess Minnie Mouse was accompanied by her pals Mickey, Goofy, Pluto, and Chip and Dale sporting Hawaiian attire. Now, character dining can be enjoyed around the Disney world.

Among the many advantages to character dining is the guaranteed chance to interact with your favorite characters. Characters come to your table while you're enjoying your meal. For young children, the intimacy of the table, rather than waiting in line in the park, can make the experience more enjoyable. Characters engage in small talk, happily sign autographs, and pose for pictures. Hugs, too.

Character dining is also a memorable way to commemorate birthdays. Ask for a celebratory birthday button when you arrive. A server may be able to arrange for cast members to sing "Happy Birthday." Or, if

OPPOSITE: **Chip or Dale might pay you a visit at Goofy's Kitchen in the Disneyland Hotel.**

PAGES 270-71: **One of the most iconic character experiences is a meal with your favorite Disney pals at Chef Mickey's in Disney's Contemporary Resort.**

you're an *Alice in Wonderland* fan, "A Very Merry Unbirthday."

These experiences are available for breakfast, lunch, and dinner, offering casual fare to fine dining. Here are some of the top events and places to book:

At **Disneyland Resort,** check out Minnie & Friends—Breakfast in the Park at the Plaza Inn; Mickey's Tales of Adventure Breakfast at Storytellers Café; Disney Princess Breakfast Adventures at Napa Rose; and Goofy's Kitchen at the Disneyland Hotel.

Walt Disney World Resort experiences include the Chip 'n' Dale's Harvest Feast at the Garden Grill Restaurant; Disney Junior Play 'n Dine Breakfast at Hollywood & Vine; Breakfast à la Art with Mickey & Friends at Topolino's Terrace—Flavors of the Riviera; Chef Mickey's Family Feast at Chef Mickey's; Dining with Donald and Friends at Tusker House Restaurant; and Story Book Dining at Artist Point with Snow White.

At **Tokyo Disney Resort,** you'll find Chef Mickey at Disney Ambassador Hotel.

Disneyland Paris offers Inventions at the Disneyland Hotel; Café Mickey at Disney Village; and Plaza Gardens Restaurant at Disneyland Park.

When visiting **Hong Kong Disneyland**, don't miss Enchanted Garden Restaurant at the Hong Kong Disneyland Hotel; Chef Mickey at Disney's Hollywood Hotel; and World of Color Restaurant and Dragon Wind at Disney Explorers Lodge.

Shanghai Disney Resort features Lumière's Kitchen at the Shanghai Disneyland Hotel and Royal Banquet Hall in Enchanted Storybook Castle. ■

SHARE OUR TABLE

The dining part of character dining is just as fun as the character interactions. Mickey Waffles are ubiquitous. However, unique selections can be found throughout the world: At Goofy's Kitchen in the Disneyland Hotel, Goofy serves his famous peanut butter pizza for breakfast. Gawrsh! At Shanghai Disneyland, Lumière's Kitchen features an array of *Beauty and the Beast*–themed desserts. Mickey Sushi is offered at the Royal Banquet Hall at Hong Kong Disneyland. Strawberry Polka-dotted Minnie Mouse Cake is for dessert at Plaza Gardens Restaurant at Disneyland Paris. And Magic Mirror's Slow-braised Pork Shank stars on the menu of Story Book Dining at Artist Point with Snow White at Walt Disney World.

A: Dopey stops by to say hi during a dinner at Artist Point in Disney's Wilderness Lodge. B: Minnie might stop by your table at Aulani Resort to show off her hula skills. C: Catch Belle with her nose stuck in a book at Napa Rose in Disney's Grand Californian Hotel & Spa. D: Princesses shouldn't leave their autograph books behind when they dine at Napa Rose in Disney's Grand Californian Hotel & Spa. E: Your little warrior will love meeting Mulan during dinner at Napa Rose. F: Join Chip and Dale at the Garden Grill in EPCOT. G: Aboard the *Disney Wonder,* dine like royalty at Tiana's Place. H: Vampirina is ready with hugs at the Disney Junior Play 'n Dine breakfast at Hollywood and Vine in Disney's Hollywood Studios.

A

D

B

C

E

F

G

H

EAT AROUND THE WORLD (IN ONE DAY)

Take Part in the International Food & Wine Festival at EPCOT

World Showcase at EPCOT has always been an epicurean destination. The international flavors, architecture, and entertainment transport guests to countries they may never visit in person. It's also the natural location for the EPCOT International Food & Wine Festival, a foodie tour that spans not only the entire park but also six continents.

This is not what some may refer to as theme park food. At Walt Disney World, the chefs take their food very seriously. They take great care with diverse cuisines, using the most authentic ingredients. Not only does it taste delicious, it looks delicious, too. This is a feast for the eyes as much as it's a feast for the stomach.

First things first. Come hungry. And thirsty.

Each "Global Marketplace"—a kiosk with a small working kitchen—offers signature dishes plus wine, beer, and cocktail pairings. No passport is needed to taste the global cuisine from A to Z: the Alps, Australia, Belgium, Brazil, Canada, China, France, Germany, Greece, India, Ireland, Italy, Japan, Kenya, Mexico, Morocco, and Spain. Outposts and other eateries offer craveables such as chicken wings, macaroni and cheese, doughnuts, lobster rolls, and burgers. Truly, there is something for everyone.

Although the food hunt is fun, detailed guidebooks are very helpful for those who want to strategize and plan in advance. EPCOT and Walt Disney

FLOWER POWER

Experience the beauty and bounty of the EPCOT International Flower & Garden Festival (between March and July). Disney topiary characters pop up throughout the park, and outdoor kitchens entice guests with fresh flavors inspired by springtime.

OPPOSITE: Dine around the world at the annual International Food & Wine Festival at EPCOT.

PAGES 276-7: The marketplaces change year to year, with crowd favorites such as Morocco, Brazil, and Australia.

World accommodate those with allergies and dietary preferences: Plant-based and vegan; gluten-, wheat-, and dairy-friendly; nonalcoholic; and other variations are available.

Bring the children. If they are not miniature gourmands, kid-friendly food is available at the permanent restaurants and quick-service spots. They'll also love to partake in Remy's Ratatouille Hide & Squeak Scavenger Hunt. Find all the Remy statuettes hidden throughout World Showcase and the Global Marketplaces and win prizes—compliments of Chef Remy. Fans of all ages will appreciate the Disney characters' appearances in the "countries" where they are from: Belle in France, Mary Poppins in England, Anna and Elsa in Norway.

Let's not forget all the magic that comes with being at EPCOT. The Eat to the Beat Concert Series features headliners from around the world. No matter what kind of music you prefer—country, Broadway, pop, R&B, or jazz—these top-name acts will keep your toes tapping. Other entertainers include Mariachi Cobre, taiko drummers, and

MORE FROM WALT

Walt conceived EPCOT to be an Experimental Prototype Community of Tomorrow. He explained: "EPCOT will be dedicated to the happiness of the people who will live, work, and play here . . . and to those who come here from around the world to visit our living showcase." Although his original idea has morphed and evolved, it is still a living showcase. And that's why it's the perfect venue for the EPCOT International Food & Wine Festival.

the Jammin' Chefs—who make syncopated music on pots and pans. The Voices of Liberty are a mainstay of The American Adventure pavilion at EPCOT. Costumed in period finery from the 1800s, the a cappella group takes the stage at America Gardens Theatre to perform the Disney Songbook.

It's easy to get tired after a long day of eating and exploring; however, don't miss the park's newest nighttime spectacular, Harmonious. Featuring an innovative combination of floating giant screens, choreographed moving fountains, lights, pyrotechnics, and lasers with a 360-degree view, it weaves Disney stories and music in a brand-new way.

There's plenty of EPCOT Food & Wine Festival merchandise to take the culinary memories home, including trading pins, hats, apparel, aprons, glassware, cookbooks, and home decor.

A park reservation and EPCOT admission are required. ∎

EAT LIKE WALT

One of the best ways to connect with Walt is to experience some of the Los Angeles restaurants he frequented between the late 1920s and 1966. Although the Brown Derby, Romanoff's, Chasen's, Hernando's Hideaway, and his breakfast favorite, Biff's (where his usual order was silver dollar pancakes), are long gone, you can still eat like Walt at the following restaurants:

THE TAM O'SHANTER

About 45 minutes north of Disneyland sits the Tam O'Shanter. Established in 1922, it remains the oldest restaurant in Los Angeles owned by the same family in the same location. Its fairy-tale exterior, in the style of the Normandy region of France, would fit right in amid any number of early Disney projects.

During the late 1920s and throughout the 1930s, Walt and his staff ate lunch there so frequently that it was referred to as the "Disney Commissary." Walt dined there so often that he purportedly knew every busboy by name. The food was in Walt's wheelhouse (he generally eschewed fancy cuisine), including hamburgers made with freshly ground beef and served on a buttered and grilled piece of white bread instead of a bun.

Today, a "Disney" table can be reserved in advance. Or request booth 35, where Walt, his team, and trusted animators ate and worked. The pegs that held hats—or a curtain when privacy was needed—are still there today.

The Tam O'Shanter serves lunch and dinner seven days a week, with brunch on the weekends. The reception area features two pieces of art that reflect Walt's admiration of the restaurant and its multigenerational owners, including one drawn by Disney Legend John Hench (Disney's

OPPOSITE: Not just a gathering place for Walt and his Imagineers, the Tam O'Shanter restaurant's Tudor-style building could fit right into one of Disney's early fairy tales.

PAGES 282-3: Clifton's Cafeteria, which opened in 1932, was one of Walt's favorite spots.

Renaissance artist and Imagineer who contributed to parks throughout the world and several films, and who was Mickey Mouse's official birthday portrait artist).

PINK'S HOT DOGS

As much as Walt loved hamburgers, he liked hot dogs, too. Mickey Mouse's very first words—voiced by Walt—were "hot dogs, hot dogs" in 1929's *The Karnival Kid*. At Disneyland, Walt reportedly paced off the distance between garbage cans based on how long it took him to eat a hot dog; he wanted to be sure there would be no reason for a guest to drop a wrapper on the ground. Whenever he visited Pink's, established in 1939, his order was always the same: a plain hot dog and a strawberry soda.

THE SMOKE HOUSE

Walt made it a habit to be at home for dinner with his family, and later when his daughters grew up, he would often eat on a TV tray in front of the television with Lilly. He did venture occasionally to fine-dining restaurants (such as Chasen's for chili), but most are gone now. The Smoke House, however, remains. Nestled among neighboring movie and television studios, everyone from executives to stars to stagehands relishes the clubhouse atmosphere. With its proximity to his studio, Walt likely may have enjoyed business lunches here. Today, you can experience the same 1940s vibe with red leather

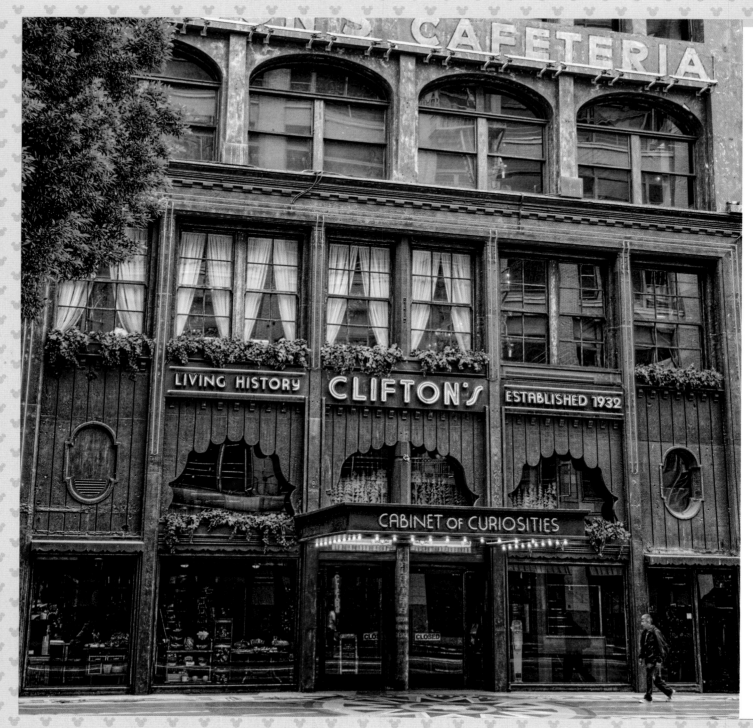

booths, walls lined with celebrity photos, and a selection of steaks and stiff cocktails.

CLIFTON'S CAFETERIA (NOW CLIFTON'S REPUBLIC)

Clifton's, a portmanteau of its founder's first and last names, was established during the Great Depression in 1931 by Clifford Clinton. Clifford was a devout Christian; he installed a flashing neon sign outside the restaurant that read "pay what you wish." Inside it was kitschy, with forest-themed decor that included towering redwood trees. After a trip to the South Seas, Clifford introduced a tropical jungle theme, which included a Polynesian grass hut and a rain effect that went off every 20 minutes. This is an example of early themed dining that may have served as an inspiration for Walt and his Enchanted Tiki Room. ■

OPPOSITE: The exterior of Clifton's is just as magical as the interior, which boasts a faux 40-foot-tall (12-m) redwood tree in the center of the restaurant.

ABOVE: The Smoke House restaurant opened in 1946 and served Walt and other luminaries, including Bob Hope and Bing Crosby.

RISE TO NEW HEIGHTS

The Tomorrowland Skyline Lounge Experience

Walt famously quipped, "Tomorrow is a heck of a thing to keep up with." But he sure tried!

Tomorrowland represents the future in science, space, technology, and transportation. When Disneyland opened in 1955, Tomorrowland was far from completed. With time running out, the voids were filled with temporary exhibits and fiberglass chairs—near the eateries and anywhere else there was an empty space, too.

The Tomorrowland Skyline Lounge Experience takes place in Walt Disney's original Magic Kingdom at what was the Tomorrowland Expo Center, previously the site of the Carousel of Progress attraction. Even if you're not a Disneyland history buff, you're going to enjoy the outdoor lounge as a respite during the evening hours of 8 to 10 p.m. If you've been waiting to ride Buzz Lightyear Astro Blasters or Space Mountain, go ahead and enjoy the attractions; you may come and go from the lounge as you please.

There is no better end to a Disney day than fireworks. And there is no better viewing than high above the crowd. If the nighttime spectacular is scheduled during your visit, you'll love the breathtaking view from the second-floor balcony.

The Skyline Lounge Experience includes a box of snacks and assorted desserts. Hot and cold beverages are also provided. You'll have everything you need to sip and savor as a temporary citizen of Tomorrowland. ■

Savor a delicious dinner, with menu options such as the Chicken Star-mesan sandwich, along with breathtaking views of Disneyland.

ENJOY THE BAO-UNTY

Delicious Disney Dim Sum at the Crystal Lotus

Part of what makes Disney special is the way it touches our hearts. So it's fitting that dim sum means "touch the heart." The traditional Chinese meal generally enjoyed for breakfast or brunch features small dumplings and buns, both steamed and fried. Like tapas, small plates are shared with everyone at the table. Tea, or "cha," is part of the communal experience.

The Crystal Lotus at the Hong Kong Disneyland Hotel is an award-winning restaurant, helmed by a renowned chef, that's worth the trip—even if you're not venturing into the park. The five basic elements—wood, fire, metal, earth, and water—are represented in the exquisite decor. Here, the fun hunt isn't for Hidden Mickeys but rather for the lotus motif sprinkled throughout the restaurant.

One of the most magical food experiences is offered exclusively at the Crystal Lotus: Disney dim sum. Inspired by Disney and Pixar characters, master chefs create adorable treats. They are sure to delight anyone, regardless of age. The selection includes Baymax Bun, Mickey's Double-Layer Turnip and Taro Pudding, Three Little Pigs Barbecue Pork Bun, *Toy Story* Little Green Men Pork and Vegetable Bun, and "Tsum Tsum" Chilled Pudding, based on the tiny stackable plush toys.

Schedule ahead for this unique opportunity, at least 24 hours in advance on weekends and 48 hours in advance Monday through Friday. ∎

As if the Crystal Lotus's decor isn't impressive enough, the dim sum—and its nod to Disney characters—will blow you away.

DISNEY LIKE AN ADULT

What are "Disney Adults"? Many things, but mostly they're adults who subscribe to Peter Pan's philosophy: Never grow up! Let's go adulting at a few Disney bars:

The Mexico pavilion in World Showcase at EPCOT has a "hidden" bar inside Plaza de los Amigos called **La Cava del Tequila.** Set in a cave, it boasts a selection of more than 200 tequilas. They offer tequila flights, plus beer and amazing margaritas. Cap off the outing by riding Gran Fiesta Tour Starring The Three Caballeros, a historic water attraction.

Built in the spirit of lodges found in U.S. national parks, the **Redwood Bar and Lounge** at Disneyland Paris is ruggedly elegant. The giant pass-through fireplace, reminiscent of the Ahwahnee hotel in Yosemite, serves as the centerpiece for the cozy lounge.

Pixar inspires the decor at Disney California Adventure's secret **Lamplight Lounge.** Fans will have plenty to ooh and aah about with the concept art, memorabilia, and treats from the Pixar Archives. Cocktails with clever names such as Over Budget and The Sequel play a starring role, along with stunning views.

Surround yourself with the spirit of the 26th president in **The Teddy Roosevelt Lounge** at Tokyo Disney-Sea. With hardwood floors, polished brass, leather club chairs, carved bears, libraries of hardbound books, and historical memorabilia, it's both lavish and patriotic. Enjoy a mint julep like Teddy did.

THIRSTY FOR ADVENTURE?

Grab a Drink at Oga's Cantina at *Star Wars: Galaxy's Edge*

Crime boss Oga Garra may be elusive; however, anyone can go to Oga's Cantina in *Star Wars: Galaxy's Edge*. There's no need to travel to a galaxy far, far away to enjoy the Batuu outpost; it's available at both Disneyland Resort and Walt Disney World Resort.

You shouldn't expect to spot the "hostess"—we recommend you don't even try. The watering hole is a gathering place for a slew of misfits, bounty hunters, smugglers, and rogue traders, none of whom are too eager to be recognized either. Keep to your business and enjoy one of Oga's cocktails. The bartenders use ingredients sourced from around the galaxy to craft libations such as Jedi Mind Trick, the Outer Rim, and Yub Nub served in a souvenir Endor mug. The beer menu includes Bad Motivator IPA and White Wampa Ale; and Hyperdrive, Jabba Juice, and Blue Bantha are nonalcoholic options. Munch on Batuu Bits, a crunchy and spicy snack mix, to go with your drink. Entertainment is provided by former Starspeeder 3000 pilot droid DJ R-3X; he spins tunes and keeps the Batuu beat. Be sure to ask your server for any specials or "secret" menu items.

Just as Han Solo could not be deterred, you should not be deterred by the strict guidelines at Oga's Cantina. Advance reservations are highly recommended. At least one person in the party must be 14 or older. Each visit is limited to 45 minutes and two drinks per person.

May the spires keep you . . . ∎

Grab a drink at Oga's Cantina, where you'll also find entertainment courtesy of droid DJ R-3X.

TAKE A TREK TO TIFFINS

Imbibe Like an Explorer With Drinks at Nomad Lounge

Nature and adventure shape everything at Tiffins, a Disney's Animal Kingdom restaurant that has served international cuisine since 2016. Each of the establishment's three dining rooms reflects the world travels of the Imagineers as they researched and created the theme park. The largest is dedicated to animal conservation and some of the wildlife that the Disney Conservation Fund is committed to protecting. This is an extension of Walt's lifelong love of animals and his own conservation legacy, which includes his *True-Life Adventures* nature documentaries (1948–1960). Art from across Asia and Africa is represented in the other two rooms.

Nomad Lounge offers a different kind of adventure than can be found in the park. It's an oasis unto itself and appeals to those prone to wanderlust. It's also thought-provoking and interactive. Within the rotunda, questions are posted about globe-trotting and the lessons learned to prompt conversation while sipping cocktails. A few examples of the queries and responses:

"What wisdom would you give to other travelers?" "Be incredibly respectful of the culture. Things may be different to you which are very commonplace to others."

"What do you always do when traveling?" "I go into travel with my eyes and ears wide open, and just try to absorb."

"What was your most unexpected discovery?" "I discovered that I could be very independent. I could go to another country by myself."

NOT A TIFFINS TYPO

It's easy to assume "Tiffins" without the possessive apostrophe is a mistake. But it isn't. Tiffin isn't a notable person. It's an Indian English word for "lunch box" or "midday meal." The restaurant name refers to the light lunch prepared for workingmen in India and the tiered containers in which the meals are served.

OPPOSITE: Tropical drinks are served on the porch at Tiffins alongside peaceful views of the river that runs through Disney's Animal Kingdom.

PAGES 296-7: Nomad Lounge offers a sense of exploration with your meal.

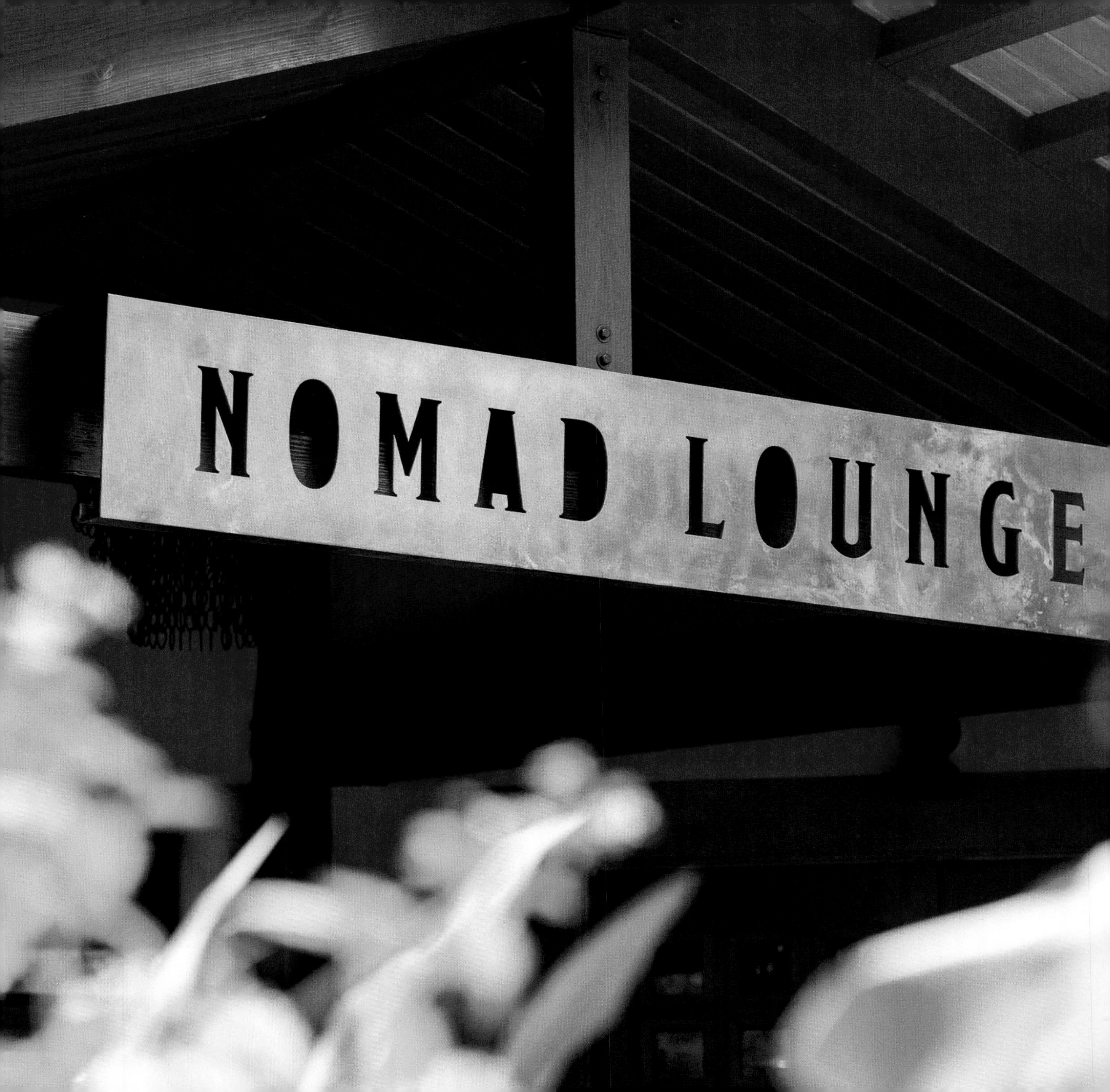
NOMAD LOUNGE

Although these are painted on the walls, guests are invited to share their reflections on "My True Tale of Adventure" cards. Purchase the cards for a nominal fee (a direct donation to the Disney Conservation Fund) from a cast member. Responses are hung on a "tag chandelier" or posted on a bulletin board; your wisdom and insight will be available for all to see.

Of course, you're here to recharge, too. A more casual setting than Tiffins, Nomad Lounge offers both indoor and outdoor seating. The menu features small plates of Asian, African, and Latin cuisine, along with wine and beer. A couple signature cocktails not to miss are the Snow Leopard Salvation, with a portion of the price donated to the conservation of these special animals, and Jenn's Tattoo, named for Jenn Gerstin, one of the Imagineers responsible for Disney's Animal Kingdom Theme Park. On a research trip for Expedition Everest—Legend of the Forbidden Mountain in 2005, Jenn found the inspiration for her first tattoo (a Tibetan snow lion) while visiting a monastery in East Asia. ∎

A SKETCH IN TIME

"Whenever I travel, I always bring a sketchbook," explains former Imagineer Joe Rohde. "There is something *very* interesting about sketching and the way it helps you to remember . . . When you sketch, you stop what you're doing, and you really, really look at the thing you are trying to draw. When you do that, it opens up the mind, and you remember. You remember very vividly the moment when you were doing the sketch." Some of Joe's sketches can be seen at Tiffins in Disney's Animal Kingdom Theme Park.

THE FIRST OF MANY

Blue Bayou: the Restaurant That Started It All

The world of Disney now has countless themed restaurants: Sci-Fi Dine-in Theater Restaurant, Columbia Harbour House, and Tusker House Restaurant at Walt Disney World; Flo's V8 Café at Disney California Adventure; Bistrot Chez Rémy at Disneyland Paris; Magellan's at Tokyo DisneySea; Tangled Tree Tavern at Shanghai Disneyland; and the Explorer's Club Restaurant at Hong Kong Disneyland. But it was Blue Bayou in Disneyland that set the bar for a fully immersive dining experience with its perennial nighttime setting.

There is something about the firstborn. Blue Bayou is still considered a prototype for the industry. Walt and his Imagineers started discussing concepts for the eatery, situated in eternal twilight, as early as 1961.

Disney Legend X Atencio, who composed the iconic "Yo Ho (A Pirate's Life for Me)" for the Pirates of the Caribbean attraction, proposed a musical number blending the bayou's natural sounds and traditional New Orleans jazz instrumentation. "[I heard] the croaking of a frog, joined by the chirping of a cricket to start the beat," he said. "Other creatures such as birds and animals and an occasional musical instrument could join in to develop the beat until a swinging melody is achieved." Although several versions of the theme were recorded, none of them were ever used. The crickets and frogs, however, were cast in the background.

Disney Legend Dick Nunis recalls that following an audience preview, Walt emphatically decided there would be no entertainment as originally planned: "In this restaurant the food is going to be the show, along with the atmosphere." Walt made another critical decision at this location. When

OPPOSITE: Blue Bayou serves up Creole-Cajun cuisine.

PAGES 300-301: Save room for dessert, with options like an eight-layer chocolate-and-hazelnut cake on the menu.

New Orleans Square was dedicated in 1966, Blue Bayou was ready but the Pirates of the Caribbean attraction wasn't. Walt wouldn't allow it to open, saying, "It's a bad show without pirate boats floating by." As a result, Walt never experienced his revolutionary restaurant; he passed away before its 1967 debut.

Walt wanted to honor the French and Spanish culinary traditions of New Orleans. Blue Bayou showcases Creole and Cajun specialties, but the Monte Cristo sandwich is the star. Although the sandwich may not be authentic to the Crescent City—it's a cousin to France's croque monsieur and believed to have originated in Southern California—it remains one of the most popular menu items at Disneyland.

Blue Bayou was the first reservation-based eatery at Disneyland. However, a table couldn't be secured by telephone. Once the park opened, guests had to physically go to the restaurant to sign up for an available time, often prompting a mad dash as soon as the gates opened.

Today, you can make your reservation online through Disney Dining. ∎

LEGEND HAS IT

Disney Legend Jim Cora recalls that in the preliminary planning of Tokyo Disneyland, Japanese stakeholders wanted an authentic American experience: They wanted Tokyo Disneyland to feel just like Disneyland in California. With that, Blue Bayou, and its menu of American fare, debuted at Tokyo Disneyland in 1983.

THE VIP TREATMENT

An Exclusive Meal in Disney's Secret Club 33

One of the most coveted and most difficult reservations to acquire is for an experience with rich history, steeped in mystery and intrigue, plus gourmet food and an extensive wine program. The secret is not so secret: Club 33.

The origin of Club 33 goes back to Disneyland Park in the 1960s. Having outgrown his private apartment on Main Street, U.S.A., Walt was planning a private club adjacent to his new apartment in New Orleans Square. Inspired by the private lounges he visited at the 1964-1965 New York World's Fair, the purpose was to entertain dignitaries, VIPs, and potential sponsors for future projects, notably Walt Disney World Resort. Walt had a private dining space planned, too: the Trophy Room, with a masculine motif and hunting trophies provided by his friends. An Audio-Animatronics vulture was mounted on the wall. Microphones were hidden in the chandeliers, placed there with Walt's playful intention to interact with his guests. The idea was basic magic: A cast member would be in an adjacent room, listening to the conversation and responding as the voice of the vulture. For instance, someone might say, "I wonder what I should have for lunch." And the vulture would answer, "Have the tomato soup!" Although the act never came to fruition, the feathered friend of the club remains perched on a grandfather clock to greet guests as they arrive. Walt's wishes for Club 33 were for an elegant experience, including cloth napkins, fine china, and classic American cuisine. Unfortunately, when it opened in 1967 Walt was not alive to raise a glass there.

Today, Club 33 is a private membership that extends throughout the Disneyland Resort, but the dining experience in New Orleans Square remains

CHEERS TO WALT

You don't need an invitation or a membership to a private club to toast Walt. Any bar will do. Bonus points for being in a Disney park, resort, or on a cruise ship. His favorite cocktail was the Scotch Mist, essentially an adult snow cone. All you need are crushed ice and one of Walt's favorite whisky brands: Black & White or Canadian Club.

OPPOSITE: Members (and their guests) are the only ones who can enter the exclusive Club 33 dining rooms throughout Disney parks and resorts.

PAGES 304-5: A staircase leads you from the Court of Angels to the entrance of Disneyland's Club 33.

at the heart. Above the winding streets of the square, guests overlook the Rivers of America while they enjoy a seasonal menu inspired by worldly cuisines with a wine pairing experience guided by certified sommeliers. In a separate room, members enjoy a private lounge experience complete with live music, casual dining, and handcrafted cocktails.

An extension of Club 33—called the 1901 Lounge—was added in 2012 at Disney California Adventure. The name pays homage to Walt's birth year. The interior represents his early experiences working with his animators and is chock-full of memorabilia.

Versions of the legendary private membership club can also be found at the Magic Kingdom, EPCOT, Disney's Hollywood Studios, and Disney's Animal Kingdom Theme Park. Each of the lounges is themed to the worldwide travels of Walt and Lillian Disney.

Tokyo Disneyland and Shanghai Disneyland Park have Club 33, as well. Oh, and if you go on Adventures by Disney's tour of China, you just might get a peek at the latter's club.

If you are not a Club 33 member, a member must accompany you or make the reservation for you. Good luck. It will be worth the wait! ∎

LEGEND HAS IT

"All of us who worked for him recognized that he loved people," Disney Legend Blaine Gibson recalls of Walt. "One time a buyer came in with some chairs they were thinking of using for the Blue Bayou restaurant . . . Walt came in and sat down on one. He looked around and said, 'We can't have these! A woman could catch her skirt on this!' Walt wanted to do what he liked, but he wanted people to be happy."

EPCOT

FARM TO PARK

A Peek Behind the Gardening Curtain: Living with the Land

EPCOT stands for Experimental Prototype Community of Tomorrow. It was Walt's dream to build a self-reliant city. Disney Legend Marty Sklar offered insight about how Walt's futuristic thinking was realized and how far ahead of the curve Walt Disney World was, even in the 1980s, decades before there was a green movement: "For me, The Land and Living Seas pavilions are the most EPCOT of all pavilions. We actually have living systems in those projects. There are new ways of growing food being demonstrated in The Land pavilion, and that was absolutely the kind of thing Walt was trying to do."

The Living with the Land attraction looks at the continuation of and commitment to Walt's legacy. The gentle cruise offers a brief history of farming. The covered boats glide past the living laboratories and carefully controlled ecosystems growing fruit and vegetables and raising fish. The Biotech Lab—where EPCOT scientists and the U.S. Department of Agriculture collaborate to find innovative ways to produce bountiful harvests to feed our planet—is seen in action behind a giant glass window. It's a lesson about how we can all learn to live responsibly with the land in the form of a carefully curated exhibit—and an attraction kids will enjoy as much as adults.

Although all of this is a "show," it's also not *just* for show. The fresh produce raised in The Land pavilion is served at restaurants throughout EPCOT. Several restaurants throughout Walt Disney World Resort use the fish—nearly 5,000 pounds (2,300 kg) each year.

Come for the holidays and see how Living with the Land gets an overlay known as "Glimmering Greenhouses" during the EPCOT Festival of the

OPPOSITE: During the Living with the Land boat ride, you'll see Disney's efforts toward sustainable farming at work.

PAGES 308-9: The produce grown in Disney's greenhouses, part of the Living with the Land tour, is used throughout the restaurants in EPCOT.

Holidays. In celebration of the season, the greenhouses become aglow with colorful lighting and delightful decorations. It's even more enchanting in the evening! With oversize ornaments, twinkling trellises, and a reindeer Mickey, it's sure to amaze you.

Another not-to-be-missed attraction is *Awesome Planet* (2020). Narrated by Ty Burrell of *Modern Family* fame, the 10-minute movie is educational and informative, with stunning imagery of Earth's spectacular beauty and scenes from Disneynature films. It's also a call to action. In partnership with the Disney Conservation Fund, the film uses in-theater effects (including wind, scents, and water) to tell the story of life on our planet and why it's vitally important to care for it.

The Land pavilion is just one example of the commitment Walt Disney World makes for not just EPCOT and the entire resort but for Mother Earth. ∎

VEGGIE VEGGIE FRUIT FRUIT

The Land pavilion once hosted an attraction that starred singing fruits and vegetables. Beginning in 1982, Kitchen Kabaret featured Audio-Animatronics figures—"seasoned performers"—in each of the four basic food groups. A most unusual souvenir emerged from that beloved attraction: vegetable plushies. A decade later, Food Rocks premiered with song parodies, including "Every Bite You Take," performed by the Refrigerator Police. As with all food, the performance had a shelf life. Food Rocks closed in 2004, and a fresh attraction—Soarin'—was added to the space.

WALT'S—AN AMERICAN RESTAURANT

Walt adored Paris, thus it's fitting that a restaurant named in his honor is located at Disneyland Paris.

Walt was a simple eater, a result of his humble upbringing. When he traveled to Europe, he'd often ship his familiar foods ahead, such as Vienna sausages, Spam, crackers, and V8 juice. Once, on a business trip for the 1964–1965 New York World's Fair, he was served lobster salad. When the meeting was finished, he turned to his team and declared, "Boy, that wasn't a very good lunch. Let's go get a cheeseburger and a chocolate shake."

The elegant establishment at Disneyland Paris is purposely reminiscent of Club 33 (see page 302). The elevator downstairs resembles the original one at Disneyland; look for the "WD" on the doors (and throughout the restaurant). The restaurant is also a photographic tribute to Walt, covering everything from his hometown of Marceline, Missouri, to Mickey Mouse to the release of *Snow White and the Seven Dwarfs* (1937). The themed dining rooms reflect the six lands of Disneyland Paris; the menu is sophisticated American and includes takes on some of Walt's favorite dishes, such as chili con carne and Waldorf salad. All these details are a tribute to Walt's life and work.

One detail on this menu deserves special recognition: the inclusion of Thelma Pearl Howard, the Disney family cook for 30 years. Walt referred to her as his "Mary Poppins." Look for her potato dish on the menu.

If you want to drink like Walt, have a Scotch Mist, his preferred cocktail (see page 302), with your meal. ∎

Feeling homesick in Disneyland Paris? Walt's— An American Restaurant offers a taste of home.

ONCE IN A NEW MOON

Celebrate Lunar New Year the Disney Way

Three Disney parks host celebrations for Lunar New Year: Hong Kong Disneyland, Shanghai Disneyland, and Disney California Adventure. The annual celebration in January and February is also known as the Spring Festival. Based on the lunar calendar, the Chinese zodiac—or shengxiao—represents 12 zodiac animals and their attributes in a 12-year cycle, although it is always the Year of the Rat, or Mouse, at Disney.

The Disney lunar festivals are a tribute to the deep traditions of Chinese, Korean, and Vietnamese cultures. They feature red and gold decorations symbolizing good fortune and happiness, keepsake merchandise, and exciting entertainment and processions.

Asian-inspired cuisine ranges from sweet, with the Lantern Whoopie Pie and Oolong Donuts, to savory, with the Mickey Chinese Hot Dog Bun and Impossible-brand Lion's Head Meatballs.

Some items have a Disney twist, others an authentic flair—but they're all delicious! Alcoholic and nonalcoholic beverages are themed, too, including the Dancing Firecracker and Green Tea Slush.

Disney California Adventure offers the Sip and Savor Pass for those who want to make the most of the epicurean adventure. At Hong Kong Disneyland, Lunar New Year is celebrated at the hotels. Special seasonal dishes celebrating Chinese New Year are available at the Crystal Lotus, Dragon Wind, World of Color, and Chart Room restaurants. ■

BEST WISHES

The Garden of the Twelve Friends transforms into the New Year's Wishing Garden during the Lunar New Year celebration at Shanghai Disneyland. Guests write their wishes for the upcoming year on special cards, which they can hang throughout the garden to usher in a year of good luck.

Celebrate Lunar New Year by stringing your Mickey-eared wish among others in Disney California Adventure Park.

EPIC EATS

It's Not a Day at Disney Without Trying These Iconic Treats

One of the first questions people ask when visiting any of the Disney parks is "What's your favorite food?" And those very popular T-shirts that declare "I'm just here for the snacks" show that food is a huge part of the parks experience. (Calories don't count on vacation, right?) These epic eats have moved way beyond hot dogs, hamburgers, and popcorn—and must be added to your Disney bucket list.

DOLE became the sponsor of Walt Disney's Enchanted Tiki Room at Disneyland in 1976. In the beginning, only fresh pineapple spears and pineapple juice were sold. DOLE Whips—a fat-free, dairy-free, and gluten-free pineapple creamy concoction—arrived at Walt Disney World in 1983. The tropical treat has expanded flavors across the parks and resorts to include lime, mango, orange, raspberry, strawberry, coconut, and watermelon, along with a seasonal fall offering of the Pumpkin Spice DOLE Whip. You can also choose options such as swirls, floats, and adult versions topped or blended with rum. DOLE Whip Day is celebrated on July 19.

Churros were first tested near the exit of the *Mark Twain* riverboat in Disneyland. Only 100 were made on that fateful day in 1985. When they were wheeled through Frontierland, guests were following the cart, and needless to say—they sold out! Variations on flavors, colors, textures, and dipping sauces were innovated more than a decade later; the churros remain fan favorites and darlings of social media.

Let's not forget the carnivores. Hickory-smoked turkey legs made their debut quietly at Walt Disney World in the late 1980s. By 2010, not only had they caught on, they were a huge hit. Each drumstick weighs in at a

OPPOSITE: Sweet and savory! Grab the Sugar Rush Pretzel from Main Street Bakery in the Magic Kingdom.

PAGES 316-7: Bring your appetite to the retro Beaches & Cream Soda Shop in Disney's Beach Club Resort, where a Kitchen Sink sundae is on the menu—eight scoops of ice cream served with every topping the shop has.

whopping one and a half pounds (0.7 kg). The meal with its own "handle" is definitely sharable—although your inner Fred Flintstone or cave dweller may not agree.

Believe it or not, it took almost 40 years to bring a fully realized, chocolate-covered ice cream bar in the shape of Mickey Mouse to Disneyland. There have been several iterations over the years, with the vanilla bar first having oblong and oval shapes, and a version with only Mickey's ears covered in chocolate. Finally, technology caught up with the mouse that started it all. The Nestlé's Mickey's Premium Ice Cream Bar was introduced in 1992.

Shave ice is a popular treat in Hawai'i. Served poolside at Aulani Resort at the Pāpālua Shave Ice stand, the dessert is customized especially for you. With flavors such as mango, pineapple, coconut, lilikoi, orange, and guava—plus options to add sweetened condensed milk or ice cream—the refreshing delight is a true taste of the Islands. It doesn't hurt that it can be served shaped like Mickey, either.

ALL CORN DOGS ARE NOT CREATED EQUAL

The Little Red Wagon corn dog cart outside the Plaza Inn at Disneyland is an homage to the first restaurant that occupied the space there, Swift's Red Wagon Inn. It's also the site of the best corn dog in Disneyland. That's because all they make there are corn dogs. Anywhere else in the park, the cooking oil is shared with other treats.

If you are screaming for ice cream, Beaches & Cream Soda Shop at Disney's Beach Club Resort at Walt Disney World usually has a line out the door. It's worth waiting for and here's why: Every day is sundae. Other offerings include cones, shakes, malts, and the Kitchen Sink—a dessert that serves four!

Pretzels and Mickey Mouse go together like Chip and Dale. The ubiquitous snack shaped like Mickey's head has been popular in the parks for decades. Purists may prefer the original soft pretzel dipped in cheese sauce or yellow mustard; however, the more adventurous might try cream cheese–filled, jalapeño cheese–filled, cinnamon, Bavarian, and even chocolate versions.

With these and so many other options, how can you possibly choose? Don't want to miss what's new and exciting? Or are you eager to find out what is seasonal? Check out the Foodie Guides published by the Disney Parks Blog. ■

OPPOSITE: **Three classics in one—the Dumbo attraction, beloved churros, and Mickey ice cream!**

ABOVE: **Award Wieners offers classic corn dogs to visitors at Disney California Adventure.**

PLAY WITH YOUR FOOD

The fascination with food in the Disney parks goes all the way back to Walt in 1955. He said, "The food's as fabulous as the fun, too." Fast-forward more than 60 years later, and it's more fun than ever! Often foodies come into the park just to eat. And to share what they're eating with the world. Blogs, websites, and social media platforms are dedicated to posting Disney food. Follow a friend, an influencer, or a hashtag to find out the latest fare, limited offerings, annual pass discounts, and craveables. This may also be your best source for finding secret menu items.

A: Come with a caveman-like appetite for an all-time park favorite, a turkey leg at the Magic Kingdom. B: One amenity not to be missed at Aulani Resort? The dipped Mickey Mouse Rice Krispies treats. C: Request that your shave ice be served in the shape of Mickey at Aulani Resort. D: Don't miss a bite from Camp Woodchuck Kitchen, especially the Mickey-shaped beef onigiri sandwich, in Tokyo Disneyland. E: Make your way to the Eggroll Wagon in Adventureland in the Magic Kingdom at Walt Disney World for unique flavors, like pizza and cheeseburger egg rolls. F: At *Star Wars: Galaxy's Edge*, head to Ronto Roasters for the crowd favorite Ronto Wrap—a grilled sausage and roasted pork delight. G: Nestlé's Mickey's Premium Ice Cream Bar, as we know it today, was introduced to the parks in 1992. H: DOLE Whips have long been a favorite throughout the Disney parks, and variations like the I Lava You Float from the Sunshine Tree Terrace in the Magic Kingdom are worth every bite.

A

B

F

G

E

H

A: Grab a snack—we recommend the Outpost Mix—from Kat Saka's Kettle at *Star Wars: Galaxy's Edge* in Disney's Hollywood Studios. B: Take a mallet, not a claw, to unveil the hidden treats in The Ganachery's chocolate Alien Piñatas at Disney Springs. C: Mighty Mist Soft Serve in Disney's Animal Kingdom is a tasty nod to *Raya and the Last Dragon* (2021). D: Duffy even gets love in the form of food—grab a bento box with Duffy and ShellieMay rice bowls from Main Street Corner Café in Hong Kong Disneyland. E: The sweets are strong with this one—a Yoda Cone from the Pineapple Lanai at Disney's Polynesian Village Resort. F: Decadent and delicious, the brownie and ice cream from Lamplight Lounge at Disney California Adventure is entirely plant-based. G: At Disney California Adventure, the Spicy Pepper Jack Dog is not to be missed at Corn Dog Castle. H: Have your own *Lady and the Tramp* (1957) romantic moment over a plate of spaghetti and meatballs at Tony's Town Square Restaurant in the Magic Kingdom. I: This ice cream-loaded taco shell comes from the Cookie Dough food truck at Disney Springs—not your average taco! J: Taste out-of-this-world shrimp aboard *Star Wars: Galactic Starcruiser*.

All food items are subject to change, and many are seasonal offerings.

BLAST OFF!

Not Your Average Astronaut Dinner at Space 220 Restaurant

Walt predicted space travel for civilians in the 1960s. Although that wasn't possible at the time, he built Rocket to the Moon at Disneyland to simulate the experience. "Although years will pass before you'll be able to take a rocket flight into space, you can do the next best thing in the meantime," he said. "Your trip will be a thrilling preview of a space voyage that many Americans may live to make."

Space 220 Restaurant is an homage to Walt's fascination with space and space travel, appropriately set in World Discovery at EPCOT and adjacent to Mission: SPACE, the astronaut simulation attraction.

The adventure begins when a crew member invites guests to step inside the restaurant's space elevator. Liftoff! Viewports offer vistas of Earth below. Whether you travel by day or night, you'll get spectacular views of EPCOT, Florida, and the eastern seaboard.

Upon arrival at the Centauri space station, diners are guided to their seats past the grow zone, a spinning wall of produce that mimics Earth's gravity and represents some of the fresh ingredients the culinary team uses. Inside the stellar 180-degree, multitiered dining room, the windows reveal an incredible view of Earth from the 220-mile-high (354-km) vantage point. Ships of every shape and size come and go, tourists enjoy space walks, kids play in the zero-g environment, and workers haul material up for the space station's ongoing construction.

With a menu offering items such as Blue Moon Cauliflower, Starry Calamari, and Slow Rotation Short Rib, it's guaranteed to be out of this world! ■

You don't have to go through astronaut training to have a dinner in space.

A PARFAIT IN PARIS

Dine at Bistrot Chez Rémy

"This much I knew. If you are what you eat, then I only want to eat the good stuff." —Remy

Ratatouille, the 2007 Disney and Pixar movie, inspired Ratatouille: The Adventure, the 2014 attraction. In this 4D experience, you shrink to the size of a rat and scurry around the kitchen—and not just any kitchen, the actual kitchen of the famous Parisian restaurant Gusteau's.

Bistrot Chez Rémy imagines that our favorite rat chef—along with his cohorts Linguini, Emile, and mentor Gusteau—have opened their own fine-dining establishment. In this immersive eatery, you'll dine atop a jam jar lid while sitting on a champagne cork chair. With your shrunken perspective, the decorative plates, bottle caps, silverware, and cocktail umbrellas all loom large.

The authentically French menu offers two- and three-course meals. In France, appetizers are known as *entrées* and include classics such as chicken rillettes and duck pâte en croûte. Mains are called *plats,* such as traditionally prepared fish and beef. Vegetarian options include *courgette* (zucchini) soup and Linguini's pasta.

Plus ratatouille, of course. Did you know that renowned American chef Thomas Keller of French Laundry fame created the recipe used specifically for the movie? Just as the fierce critic Anton Ego was impressed, so will you be.

Desserts range from cheese—a favorite finisher in France—to tarte tatin to mousse (not mouse!) au chocolat.

Bon appetit! Bistrot Chez Rémy awaits you. ∎

At Bistrot Chez Rémy, the decor is larger than life, making you feel rat-size by comparison.

CUISINE FIT FOR A KING & QUEEN

Find Your Spot at the Chef's Table at Victoria & Albert's

It's like the seat behind home plate at the World Series or orchestra center for the hottest Broadway show—only with haute cuisine and exquisite wines.

Victoria & Albert's, in Disney's Grand Floridian Resort & Spa, is considered the premier restaurant at Walt Disney World Resort. And one lucky party of up to eight guests per evening can enjoy the Chef's Table—an exclusive experience in the kitchen of Victoria & Albert's.

This culinary adventure begins with a champagne toast with the chef. Then sit back, relax, and enjoy the ride. Each tasting menu is unique and may contain as many as 11 courses, all influenced by the season. Enjoy luxurious offerings, too, such as caviar, Maine lobster, and Japanese beef.

During your three-hour feast, the culinary team will interact with you to explain the dishes and the inspiration behind them. This is the front row of a show! Any serious foodie will delight in watching the inner workings of the kitchen and the symphony of the chefs as they prepare meals for the entire restaurant. Sommeliers will be at the ready to pair your degustation with the perfect wines.

Recognized with many prestigious awards, including the Forbes Travel Guide Five-Star Award, Wine Spectator Best of Award of Excellence, and AAA Five Diamond Award, Victoria & Albert's is truly fine dining at its best. In keeping with the elegant service and atmosphere, adhere to the restaurant's dress code. ∎

Watch the chefs in action while dining on tasty menu options from Victoria & Albert's, such as this smoked buffalo served with a salad of beets, hearts of palm, and Florida orange vinaigrette.

POP-ULAR POPCORN

Put This on Your *Bucket* List

You may have walked past the carts at Disneyland or ordered popcorn without even noticing the tiny characters that are rotating the canisters attached to a faux steam pump. They've been affectionately called "toastie-roasties" (originally named "Tosty Rosty" by Cretors and Company, the inventor of the original popcorn machines used at Disneyland) and are themed to the land in which they perform. For instance, in Tomorrowland, you'll find a spaceman, a nod to the in-park character of Walt's era, and an abominable snowman, a feature of the nearby Matterhorn Bobsleds. Discovering the rest is up to you; it's all part of the fun!

Another treasure hunt that happens at all the Disney parks involves popcorn—collecting the buckets. Lines to purchase the popcorn buckets (often sold in limited quantities and sometimes available only to annual pass holders) occasionally exceed the wait times for the most popular rides. The buckets are themed to characters, lands, movies, holidays, attractions, and blasts from the past. Many consider the two-for-one package of a snack and a collectible the best park souvenir. (You may request your popcorn in a box if you want to keep your collectible pristine.) Once home, some collectors repurpose the empty vessels for purses and lunch boxes.

Want to create your own custom popcorn? Visit the Kernel Kitchen at the Main Street Confectionery in the Magic Kingdom. Personalize your sweet and savory treat by choosing from four flavors of popcorn—caramel, rainbow fruit, buttery, or cheddar—and add an assortment of candies and, for an extra pop, a drizzle of syrup. ■

Lively pint-size figurines churn out popcorn to perfection throughout Disneyland and Hong Kong Disneyland.

CHAPTER FIVE

WHEN YOU WISH UPON A STAR

Once-in-a-Lifetime Splurges

A stay in the Adventureland Suite at the Disneyland Hotel (page 358) is the ultimate in luxury.

A GOOD NIGHT

See the Park After Dark

Walt was known to gallivant about Disneyland early in the morning, long before the park opened to the public. However, evenings held charm for him, too: "You know, this is one of my favorite times of day here. Just about sundown. I like to be around when the lights come on. Seems like a new kind of magic takes over in Disneyland after dark."

Today, Disneyland After Dark is a separately ticketed, after-hours event. On select nights after they close to the general public, Disneyland Park and Disney California Adventure Park offer fun festivities you can't experience during regular daytime visits. "Nite" events—held at Disney California Adventure—are an homage to an earlier era at Disneyland when special evening gatherings such as Grad Nite and Date Nite took place.

The evening extravaganzas offer guests of all ages character experiences, photo opportunities, dancing, themed menu selections, entertainment, commemorative keepsakes, and merchandise. Select attractions—usually with shorter wait times—are available, too. Costumes, themed attire, and dress-up are encouraged. No theme park reservation is required, and guests may enter the park as early as 6 p.m. Examples of previous after-hours events include:

Star Wars Nite spans from Batuu to Tomorrowland, featuring a Galactic Dance Party, the March of the First Order with Captain Phasma and her elite unit of Stormtroopers, a pyrotechnic *Star Wars* spectacle, and plenty of glowing lightsabers. Whether you identify with the dark side or the light side of the force, are Yoda ready to party?

OPPOSITE: For a night on the town, visit the House of Blues Orlando in Disney Springs.

PAGES 336-7: Guests might meet their favorite wicked character during Villains Nite.

Sweethearts Nite takes place in February, the month of Valentine's Day, and is a celebration of *amour* of all kinds. Disney love songs are piped through the park and couples from beloved Disney movies appear in all the lands. Attend the Royal Ball at "it's a small world" and watch Disney lovebirds waltz to the Royal Band. Take a romantic moonlit jazz cruise on the *Mark Twain* or be serenaded by the Dapper Dans on Main Street, U.S.A. It's an evening with a whole Lava love.

Feeling nasty like Ursula? Is Cruella your hero? Are you all about the flex like Gaston? Then pack your poison for **Villains Nite.** It's good to be bad at Disney California Adventure Park's sinister soiree. Get down—way down—on the dance floor with Hades at the Underworld Dance Party; bring your voice for a Seaside Sing-Along with our favorite sea witch; and watch the macabre musical at the Bald Mountain Night Club hosted by Dr. Terminus with guest stars Queen of Hearts, Mother Gothel, and other misfits. It's Lotso-frightful fun! ■

GRAD NITE REUNION

Grad Nite at Disneyland used to be exclusively for those who recently received a diploma, but now anyone can experience that carefree feeling of finishing high school. The reunion party at Disney California Adventure celebrates the past six decades. Dust off that letterman jacket—everyone is encouraged to dress in their favorite retro fashions—and get in the school spirit with unique cafeteria-inspired food, dance parties, and a pep rally.

GO CASTLE-HOPPING

Visit All Six Disney Castles Around the World

S leeping Beauty Castle, the crown jewel of Disneyland, debuted in 1955 and is the only Disney castle created by Walt Disney. He wanted his castle to be friendly; standing at 77 feet (23 m) above the moat, it was built on a smaller scale. Initially referred to as a medieval castle and the Fantasyland Castle, Walt eventually settled on Sleeping Beauty Castle to promote his upcoming film, which premiered more than three years after Disneyland opened.

The sheer size of **Cinderella Castle** in the Magic Kingdom at Walt Disney World distinguishes it from its West Coast counterpart. The noble landmark stands at 189 feet (58 m) and features towering spires and ornate turrets. Disney Legend Herb Ryman, who also contributed to Sleeping Beauty Castle, was the chief designer. Inspirations included the palaces of Fontainebleau and Versailles, the châteaus of Chenonceau, Chambord, and Chaumont—and the 1950 film *Cinderella* of course.

From the outside, **Cinderella Castle** at Tokyo Disneyland is nearly identical to the one in the Magic Kingdom. But step inside and you'll see that Cinderella's Fairy Tale Hall sets them apart. In the walk-through attraction, Cinderella and Prince Charming invite their guests to explore the castle's artworks and dioramas.

Le Château de la Belle au Bois Dormant at Disneyland Paris is truly a fairy-tale castle. The castle and its surroundings were based on Disney Legend Eyvind Earle's design work on 1959's *Sleeping Beauty*. It was also inspired by fictional palaces and real French castles. With soaring spires,

OPPOSITE: Enchanted Storybook Castle at Shanghai Disneyland is the tallest and largest Disney castle ever built.

PAGES 340-41: Le Château de la Belle au Bois Dormant at Disneyland Paris boasts loads of surprises, including square-shaped hedges and a dragon in its cellar (page 40).

regal royal blue roofs, tapestries, and stained glass windows, it is both magical and *magnifique!* Square trees reminiscent of those in the film add to the enchantment.

Inspired by 13 tales of beloved Disney princesses and queens, the **Castle of Magical Dreams** at Hong Kong Disneyland was the first Disney castle to shift its focus from one princess to multiple heroines. The diversity and unique stories of the familiar heroines are told in clever architectural elements. The finials atop the spires are icons unique to those characters. Merida has a bow and arrow; Pocahontas has her faithful companion Flit the hummingbird. The colors of the towers represent the heroines, too. Jasmine's, for instance, is turquoise, a nod to her signature outfit. Other accents help interpret the heroines, such as the cherry blossoms embossed on Mulan's tower. Aurora's is the highest, a tribute to *Sleeping Beauty* (1959) and Walt's original castle. Inside, the three good fairies spread sparkly magic dust as

LEGEND HAS IT

Inside the entry passage of Cinderella Castle in the Magic Kingdom are five mosaics depicting Cinderella's story. Designed by Disney Legend Dorothea Redmond, the faces of Cinderella's stepsisters feature a color representative of their reactions as they behold Cinderella trying on the glass slipper: Look for one "green with envy" and another "red with rage." The 15-by-10-foot (4.6-by-3-m) panels were created with a million pieces of multicolored Italian glass, real silver, and 14-karat gold.

they lead the way to the royal rotunda and its 9,000 points of shimmering light above.

Enchanted Storybook Castle at Shanghai Disneyland is the tallest, largest, and most complex Disney castle ever built. Four mosaic murals showcase princesses in all four seasons, featuring Rapunzel, Tiana, Merida, Elsa, and Anna. Snow White gets her tribute with Once Upon a Time, an interactive walk-through attraction. The adventure takes you through the Magic Mirror portal and into an enchanted dimension where forests grow, creatures talk, and fairy tales come true. Guests can also travel through the castle's caverns aboard boats in Voyage to the Crystal Grotto.

It's considered an amazing accomplishment to visit all six Disney castles around the world! ∎

RISE AND SHINE

Take Part in Almsgiving During a Tour of Luang Prabang

Experience the beauty, history, and magic of Vietnam, Laos, and Cambodia. The 12-day tour with Adventures by Disney melds travel with a celebration of each country's traditions, including martial arts, regional cuisines, and religious practices.

Three days of the journey are spent in Luang Prabang, a UNESCO World Heritage site considered to be the cultural heart of Laos and known for its forests, mountains, waterfalls, and Buddhist temples. Rice is a staple here and although it is simple, the process of growing it is not; learn about the 13 stages of rice production at a local community farm. Is anything more relaxing than the sound of cascading water? Visit Kuang Si Falls for a midday retreat.

Rise and shine! The last morning in Luang Prabang is one of Adventures by Disney's most special opportunities: Participate in the ancient Buddhist alms-offering ceremony. A "must-do" on many travelers' lists, meet saffron-robed monks and give them offerings of sticky rice and other foods during this sacred ritual, one that has been occurring for centuries. As the monks amble through the ancient town, food is presented to them by the community (and you)—a gesture of respect.

After almsgiving, hike to Mount Phousi, also known as the "holy mountain." As you ascend, you'll pass Buddha statues and colorful flowers before summiting to panoramic views. Next, you'll continue your Disney adventures in Cambodia, where you'll explore Angkor—also a UNESCO World Heritage site—home to Angkor Wat, the most famed of all of Cambodia's temples, so much so that it appears on the nation's flag. ∎

Participate in almsgiving—offering food to monks at sunrise—during a guided trip to Laos.

WALK IN WALT'S FOOTSTEPS

Disneyland is one of the best places in the world to experience the spirit of Walt Disney. It is the only Disney theme park in the world in which Walt worked, played, and occasionally slept. His imprint remains firmly intact at his original Magic Kingdom.

The Walk in Walt's Footsteps guided group tour is an opportunity to traverse the park with an expert. Enhancing the experience are small individual radios that play excerpts of Walt detailing his vision. The combination of hearing Walt's voice while standing at the site he is describing is pure magic. Learn about the attractions he helped create and the stories behind them.

Perhaps the most coveted benefit of this tour—offered occasionally and never announced in advance—is the opportunity to see Walt's private apartment above the fire station. (There used to be an authentic fireman's pole, but it was removed and the hole sealed when children tried shimmying up it to get inside.) Entering from backstage and up the stairs, the compact Victorian-themed residence features two couches that double as daybeds, a small galley kitchen, and a bathroom with a shower. The adjacent balcony gave Walt and his guests a bird's-eye view of passing parades and the daily flag retreat ceremony (page 48).

No matter what the surprises and delights are the day of your tour, you'll leave having a deeper appreciation of the world's master showman and his personal playground.

Those looking for a self-guided tour of Walt's Disneyland can explore the attractions he helped create, beginning with Walt Disney's Enchanted

OPPOSITE: VIP tour guides take you behind the scenes of Disneyland to show you Walt's impact on the park.

PAGES 348-9: Walt looks over a model of Disneyland with Imagineer and Disney Legend Bill Martin (front) and executive and son-in-law Robert "Bob" Brown (center).

Tiki Room. When it opened in 1963, it was his first Audio-Animatronics attraction, and it remains the only attraction at Disneyland with his name on it. The Pirates of the Caribbean attraction has a unique Walt contribution. The ride's drop was not intended as a thrill; its purpose was to get the boats under the railroad tracks to the show building beyond the berm. His Imagineers suggested one big drop; however, it was Walt's idea to add a second drop as a surprise. The *Mark Twain* riverboat was very special to Walt. As a boy, he dreamed of sailing the Mississippi like his hero Mark Twain; the inaugural voyage was on the occasion of his 30th wedding anniversary.

Don't pass by Great Moments with Mr. Lincoln in Town Square's Opera House. See the show Walt championed about his favorite president. He felt all Americans should know the legacy of Lincoln, so much so that he offered free admission to the attraction for guests 17 and younger.

Over in Fantasyland, find Peter Pan's Flight. Walt's inspiration for the Opening Day attraction goes back to seeing *Peter Pan* as a young boy in Marceline, Missouri. Enamored by the boy who never grows up, he also played the title role in a school play.

Continue your tour with a hop over to Tom Sawyer Island, an attraction Walt designed all by himself. And don't miss the Grand Circle Tour aboard Walt's trains.

To learn more about the attractions Walt championed, check out the Disneyland app. ■

HIS-TOUR-Y

Walt introduced tour guides to Disneyland to be his representatives in the park. Among early costuming options were equestrian-style garments that may have been inspired by Walt's enjoyment of horse racing. Walt quipped, "This is a tour guide costume, sort of a jockey-like costume with a riding crop. And sometimes they are referred to as guest jockeys." The recognizable red, white, and blue Royal Stewart tartan plaid pattern worn now is reminiscent of the servers' uniforms at one of Walt's favorite restaurants, the Tam O'Shanter (page 280).

A: Cast members are the expert leaders who show you the inner workings of Disneyland and the best of Walt's contributions. B: On a VIP tour, you might get an exclusive look at Walt and Lillian's apartment above the firehouse. C: The Casey Jr. Circus Train takes you through mini versions of fairy-tale locales from classic Disney movies. D: The whole family will enjoy VIP tours of park sites and attractions. E: A model of the nation's Capitol Building is on display in the lobby of Great Moments with Mr. Lincoln. F: Mark Twain was one of Walt's personal heroes, so it was no surprise when he named the park's riverboat *Mark Twain*. G: A tour of a different kind: The Disney Youth Education Series offers unique learning experiences inside Disney parks. H: Guides greet guests for a day of fun following in Walt's footsteps around Disneyland.

A

D

B

C

E

F

G

GUIDED TOUR Guests

Please Meet
Your Tour Guide Here

H

DISNEY'S POLYNESIAN VILLAGE RESORT

YOU WON'T BE BORA-ED IN THESE BUNGALOWS

The Polynesian was one of two original resorts that opened with Walt Disney World on October 1, 1971. The inspiration for the lush tropical paradise came from Walt's trips to the South Seas and various other oceanic regions. The resort is built around the Great Ceremonial House, which was designed to resemble a Tahitian royal lodge, with a lobby that welcomes 'ohana (which, as Stitch reminds us, means "family"). The guest rooms are spread across several longhouses. Specialties from the South Pacific, Asian-infused dishes, and American classics are served in the restaurants for breakfast, lunch, and dinner. Plus DOLE Whips for dessert! Park-hoppers will love that the resort has its own Monorail station.

In 2015, Disney's first over-the-water bungalows were added. The two-bedroom bungalows will make you feel like you're on an island getaway with all the comforts of home (we're talking a kitchen, washer and dryer, and separate rooms). Replete with unobstructed views of the Seven Seas Lagoon, each of the Bora Bora bungalows comes with a personal plunge pool on a private deck. And the magic doesn't end there: Every evening, watch the water come to life during the nighttime water parade from the comfort of your Disney home.

You're going to lava it!

CALIFORNIA DREAMIN'

Signature Disney Dining on Top of the World

Disney's Contemporary Resort debuted in 1971 on the same day Walt Disney World opened to the public. The unique A-frame architecture was built like an egg crate in cooperation with U.S. Steel, and each individual guest room was constructed and furnished elsewhere and then slid into the framework of the hotel with giant cranes. With the Monorail gliding through it and the 90-foot-high (27-m) mosaic mural designed by Disney Legend Mary Blair in the Grand Canyon Concourse, it was an impressive spectacle at the time.

Top of the World—the signature restaurant on the 15th floor—was another star of the property. Along with floor-to-ceiling windows and magnificent views of the Magic Kingdom, the venue showcased a lively dinner show twice nightly, complete with headliner entertainment. Later, in 1981, "Broadway at the Top" premiered featuring artists belting show tunes.

When California Grill took the restaurant's place in 1995, the focus changed to the gourmet cuisine of the Golden State—a concentration on fresh, seasonal ingredients, plus forward-thinking preparation. A table at California Grill remains one of the most coveted dining experiences at Walt Disney World.

Also notable are its renowned wine list, onstage kitchen, and breathtaking views of the Seven Seas Lagoon, Florida woodland, and Cinderella Castle. As if this all isn't an adventure in itself, California Grill offers a unique view of the fireworks extravaganza at the Magic Kingdom, including piped-in music. Befitting this fine venue, there is a dress code, and advance reservations are highly recommended. ∎

The food at California Grill is just as good as the restaurant's views over the Magic Kingdom.

DELICIOUS DISNEY

Disney dining has evolved since the first "fancy" restaurant at Disneyland. Restaurants throughout the parks and resorts have gone on to win AAA Five Diamond Awards and receive recognitions for excellence from Zagat, Forbes Travel Guide, and *Wine Spectator*, and Disney chefs have been nominated for James Beard Foundation Awards. Disney uses the term "signature dining" to identify top-tier restaurants. They offer high-end cuisine, unparalleled service, enchanting atmosphere, top-notch wine lists, and upscale experiences—all seasoned with pixie dust and finished with magic!

A: The Storytellers Café in Disney's Grand Californian Hotel & Spa is a great spot for American fare and a chance to meet Disneyland characters. B: At Jiko—The Cooking Place restaurant, inside Disney's Animal Kingdom Lodge, you'll find tasty fare like Young Cedar Creek clam malata. C: Aboard the *Disney Wonder,* grab a bite at Tiana's Place. D: It's all five stars for the Ratatouille at Bistrot Chez Rémy in Disneyland Paris. E: Step back in time at Victoria's Home-Style Restaurant in Disneyland Paris. F: Try the plant-based African Drum Beets dessert at Jiko in Disney's Animal Kingdom Lodge. G: Fit for kings and queens—and their princes and princesses, too—the Royal Banquet Hall in Shanghai Disney Resort is a worthwhile dinner experience. H: Steamed buns get a playful twist at Chef Mickey in Hong Kong Disneyland's Hollywood Hotel.

A

D

B

C

E

F

G

H

THE SUITE LIFE

Spend a Night Immersed in the Magic

Staying late in the park is always fun, but you will likely be heading back to the Disneyland Hotel early if you've scored one of their signature suites.

Tinker Bell personally greets you in the **Fairy Tale Suite.** Follow her pixie dust as she illuminates a crystal castle encased in the wall. The elegant room features a marble foyer, floor-to-ceiling windows, an exquisite canopy bed, and a hand-cut mosaic of Sleeping Beauty Castle.

Inspired by the wildest attraction in the wilderness—Big Thunder Mountain Railroad—the **Big Thunder Suite** is 1,400 square feet (130 sq m) of movie rustic fun. Wolves howl when the doorbell is pushed, and a runaway mine train screeches in the "Fool's Gold" foyer. If you're looking for more ambience, a button on the wall triggers the attraction's sound effects. Don't miss the nugget in the living room: A gold miner's "portrait" changes as he goes about his daily duties.

You'll be singing "Yo Ho (A Pirate's Life for Me)" as soon as you enter the **Pirates of the Caribbean Suite.** Based on the film franchise and the iconic attraction, the landlubber accommodations include Captain's Quarters and a nautically themed bedroom for the younger mateys. A locked display exhibits a treasure trove of memorabilia, including a replica of Jack Sparrow's revolver, rare pirate figurines, and Davy Jones' "Dead Man's Chest."

A luxurious safari awaits in the **Adventureland Suite.** The main bedroom is fashioned as a lodge, complete with a grotto in the bathroom and lightning and rainforest sound effects. Young explorers sleep in a "tent." Authentic jungle sounds and a hidden closet add to the adventure. ∎

Disneyland Hotel's Fairy Tale Suite is fit for royalty.

CINDERELLA CASTLE SUITE

An overnight stay in the Cinderella Castle Suite at the Magic Kingdom is more coveted than an invitation to the ball. The private royal residence is not offered to public tours, and a stay here is very rare. When you enter the royal Bed Chamber, you'll see a carved C above the beds. The view of the Magic Kingdom from the stained glass windows is breathtaking; each window tells a part of Cinderella's story, as does the movie that plays in the Magic Mirror. The Bath Chamber features chandeliers that resemble crowns and large sink basins to remind Cinderella of her humble days. The soaking tub is surrounded by three mosaics and is lit from above with twinkling stars. When you check out (in the morning, not midnight), a glass slipper is presented as a memento.

A: A stay in the Cinderella Castle Suite might also mean meeting the princess herself. B: Cozy up by the fireplace and watch *Cinderella* (1950) while living like royalty. C: Tuck yourself in with cozy royal bedding. D: The round sitting room in the Cinderella Castle Suite is the perfect place to rest your feet after a day in the Magic Kingdom. E: Stained glass windows add colorful touches to the Bath Chamber. F: Also in Cinderella Castle, you'll pass a suit of armor on your way to dinner at Cinderella's Royal Table. G: Very lucky families might receive an elusive invitation to stay in the Cinderella Castle Suite. H: While soaking in the Jacuzzi-style tub, gaze at the stars in the illuminated ceiling above you.

A

D

B

C

E

F

G

H

SURF'S UP

Take a "Hawaiian Roller Coaster Ride"

The legend of Disney's Typhoon Lagoon Water Park at Walt Disney World has a sensational storm whipping across a mythical paradise, leaving destruction—Disney style—in its wake: shipwrecks, surfboards stuck in palm trees, and a shrimp boat (which operated from nearby Safen Sound) perched precariously atop a volcanic mountain. After the tempest cleared, a tropical paradise was left in its wake and an aqua playland was created in its midst. A lazy river and waterslides amuse; however, the real thrills are found in North America's largest outdoor wave pool.

Mickey Mouse, Goofy, and Stitch ride the waves. Do you? At Typhoon Lagoon, you can hang ten with the best of them! The water park offers private instruction to beginners on select days before it opens to the public. Regardless of your experience, professional surf instructors will have you riding up to six-foot (1.8-m) waves by the end of the lesson. Equipment and digital photography are included with your totally awesome adventure. Classes are approximately two and a half hours long and limited to 12 guests age eight and older.

Experienced shredders can shoot the curl before the park opens or after it closes. Limited to 25 guests, each three-hour session comes with 100 waves broken into sets of 25. While catching the perfect wave in the world-class surf, you get to choose if they break left or right. Before you paddle out, power up with an optional breakfast package. Want bragging rights? Spectators are allowed and professional photographers are available. Cowabunga! ■

Hang ten with a surf lesson at Disney's Typhoon Lagoon Water Park.

DRIVE RIGHT IN

What can drive on land, float on water, and taxi you around Lake Buena Vista? An Amphicar! The Boathouse Orlando in Disney Springs is the only place in the world that offers commercial guided tours in a vintage Amphicar, a rare vehicle that operates on land and in water, first brought to market in 1961 (fewer than 400 exist today). The adventure begins when your captain welcomes you into the unique vehicle. After securing the watertight doors, the captain drives down the ramp and the vehicle splashes dramatically into the water for a 20-minute cruise highlighting the landmarks and panoramic vistas of Disney Springs.

BEYOND DELUXE

A Five-Star Stay at the Four Seasons Orlando

Nestled in an exclusive neighborhood close to the Magic Kingdom, Disney's Hollywood Studios, EPCOT, and Disney's Animal Kingdom parks, the Four Seasons in Orlando is a luxury option for the most discerning Disney fan. It's just far enough away from the hustle and bustle to feel like the oasis it is. The accommodations and amenities are everything you'd expect at a AAA Five Diamond Resort. Be pampered in the spa and salon. Hit the links on the resort's championship golf course. Play tennis, bocce, and sand volleyball, or shoot hoops. No need to leave the resort to eat; there are world-class dining options, both formal and casual.

And the hotel comes with all the perks you'd expect from a Walt Disney World property—and more: a dedicated concierge with cast members ready to assist with tickets and reservations, providing all the planning and organization you'll need for a seamless stay; early theme park entry; complimentary transportation; Goofy & His Pals character breakfasts; gift shops; a private five-acre (2-ha) water park with waterslides and a lazy river; a boutique with prince and princess costumes; "dive-in" movies; and nightly Magic Kingdom fireworks viewed from the rooftop restaurant.

To top it off, you can enjoy private character dining with no lines and no waiting. Enjoy one-on-one time with beloved Disney characters. Truly a magical opportunity!

Still looking to impress your young ones? The Four Seasons takes "room service" to a whole new level with personalized in-room decorations for kids, such as play tents and themed toys. It's hard to imagine a Disney dream that the Four Seasons in Orlando can't make come true. ■

The Four Seasons Orlando at Walt Disney World Resort offers a retreat for families and couples looking for an elegant getaway.

BROTHERLY LOVE

Book Your Passage in a Walter E. Disney or Roy O. Disney Suite

---

Walt and his family began going on cruises in the mid-1930s. Besides being one of the primary methods of international passage at the time, boat travel offered a pace and lifestyle that were pleasing to hardworking Walt. His daughter Diane remarked that he liked to "enjoy unstructured time on board, so different than the rigors of the studio, and kept busy with the typical activities of passenger cruises, from shuffleboard to medicine ball workouts."

Walt's brother Roy was a fan of the high seas, too. He and his wife, Edna, joined Walt and Lilly on a 1935 transatlantic cruise aboard the *Normandie*, the longest and fastest vessel at the time.

Now you can travel in Disney brothers style aboard Disney Cruise Line with the Walter E. and Roy O. Disney Suites available on the *Dream, Fantasy, Magic,* and *Wonder* ships. Their grand style is reminiscent of cabins in the 1930s and '40s, with polished wood and elegant streamlined furniture. Although the layouts are quite similar and include tributes to their fabled partnership— such as cameras and books that inspired their classics—the personal touches of photographs and other mementos in the palatial staterooms reflect the individuals.

Both feature everything you'll need to relax and entertain: two bedrooms, a kitchen with a refrigerator, a butler's pantry, an expansive salonlike living room, sweeping verandas (with a Jacuzzi in some cases), dedicated concierge service, and a touch of pixie dust.

Perks unique to this experience are being among the very first to board the ship and bragging rights for life. ∎

Sail in luxury while staying in the palatial Roy O. Disney Suite aboard the *Disney Dream*.

SO SUITE

W alt and Lilly first visited Hawai'i in 1934. Although Walt received many social invitations on that trip, he rejected them all, saying, "I don't want to do anything except to lie on the beach in the sun and wiggle my toes in the sand."

In the summer of 1939, Walt and Lilly returned to Hawai'i with Walt's brother Roy and Roy's wife, Edna. They traveled to Honolulu on the S.S. *Lurline* and stayed in Waikiki. Walt visited the island three more times after that trip; island life agreed with him.

See what Walt cherished most about Hawai'i by booking a suite at Aulani, A Disney Resort & Spa. Or find paradise on the mainland in other suites throughout Disney that bring Walt's legacy of magic and wonder to life.

A: Try scuba diving with the help of instructors in the private Rainbow Reef at Aulani, A Disney Resort & Spa. B: The Metro Pool at Disneyland Paris's Hotel New York—The Art of Marvel has an indoor and outdoor heated pool and a kids' area. C: Feel at home on the savanna with a villa at Disney's Animal Kingdom Lodge. D: The views are as magical as the experiences at Aulani, A Disney Resort & Spa in Ko Olina, Hawai'i. E: Savanna-view rooms at Animal Kingdom Lodge offer dreamscapes where animals may greet you in the morning. F: Get waterfront views during your stay in the Treehouse Villas at Disney's Saratoga Springs Resort & Spa. G: Rooms at the Art of Animation Resort at Walt Disney World bring your favorite characters and drawings to life. H: Disney's Wilderness Lodge at Walt Disney World pays homage to the national parks and the great outdoors.

A

D

B

C

E

F

G

H

THE KEYS TO THE KINGDOM

We like to think of this as a splurge not just because of the additional fee, but because it's a splurge with time, too. At five hours, Disney's Keys to the Kingdom Tour is a solid portion of your day in the Magic Kingdom; however, we promise you it will be well worth it to gain backstage access to legendary hidden areas.

Explore the history of the original Walt Disney World theme park, beginning with the man behind the mouse and "Project X" (a term used to keep the Disney identity secret while purchasing land near Orlando). You'll gain insight into Walt's thought process as he was designing the park and how Roy completed his brother's dream after he passed away.

Do you like knowing secrets you can use to impress your fellow park fans? Plenty of those will be revealed on the tour, including some about your favorite attractions and the location of Hidden Mickeys (page 136). Curious if it's fact or fiction that the Magic Kingdom is on the second floor of a massive structure and that a warren of tunnels lies beneath it? Well, it's true, and you'll see it for yourself! Called the Utilidor, the underground system is how cast members, deliveries and supplies, and vehicles travel throughout the park unseen—garbage, too, the management of which was very important to Walt. You may not learn this on your tour, but you are learning it here: Walt helped to popularize the swinging-door trash cans ubiquitous in all the Disney parks. He didn't want guests lifting lids and seeing rubbish, all part of his master plan for a pristine park.

OPPOSITE: Walt Disney shows a miniature version of the Carousel of Progress at the 1964–1965 New York World's Fair.

PAGES 374–5: The Tomorrowland Transit Authority PeopleMover takes guests behind the scenes of attractions such as Space Mountain and Buzz Lightyear's Space Ranger Spin.

With all the walking and talking, you'll surely work up an appetite. Lunch is included, along with an exclusive keepsake. This extraordinary experience is for guests 16 years and older.

Looking for a shorter guided tour? The Walt Disney: Marceline to Magic Kingdom Tour is a lighter alternative, yet sure to delight any Disney fan. The behind-the-scenes excursion discusses Walt's upbringing in Marceline, Missouri (page 84), and how it affected his personal and professional life. He was known to repeat, "To tell the truth, more things of importance happened to me in Marceline than have happened since—or are likely to in the future."

You'll also discover how the 1964–1965 New York World's Fair led to the design and development of attractions featured in the Magic Kingdom.

If you can't join an official tour, make your own by visiting two iconic Walt attractions. Walt was involved with every aspect of the Carousel of Progress, which examines the American family and the role technology plays in our daily lives. He said about the People-Mover and his plan to improve transportation, "No use talking about the future unless you build it. Someday, there'll be PeopleMovers like this around every city, and in every airport." These historic attractions are only available at Walt Disney World. ∎

AROUND THE WORLD (AND PARKS) IN 24 DAYS

Alongside a team of National Geographic experts, embark on a globe-trotting expedition aboard a privately chartered Boeing 757. Instead of having the standard 233 passenger seats, the plane is lavishly reconfigured with two-by-two, VIP-style leather seating for 75 travelers.

The once-in-a-lifetime adventure is more than three weeks long and worth the price tag: You'll jet off to 12 countries, from Peru to Australia to Jordan. Along the way, you'll see UNESCO World Heritage sites, including Angkor, Rapa Nui National Park, and the Taj Mahal.

Travelers should be prepared for active days: Tours include hiking and snorkeling, as well as leisurely exploits like safari drives and light city walking tours. At every stop—and aboard the plane—National Geographic experts offer the unique heritage and history of each of these remarkable destinations.

Want another magical adventure of a lifetime? A new Adventures by Disney private jet trip takes you to all 12 Disney parks, three Disney studios, and three iconic landmarks: the Taj Mahal, the Pyramids at Giza, and the Eiffel Tower. Travelers will spend 24 days flying in luxury on a specially configured Boeing 757 from Orlando to Paris to Tokyo. Guests will get VIP tours of the parks and studios, plus insider extras including a junk boat dinner cruise in Hong Kong and a visit to Disney's Flavor Lab, where they'll have a backstage pass to the magic that chefs dream up for Disney diners around the world.

ROLL OUT THE RED CARPET

Get a Backstage Pass to All the Fun

For an entirely personalized experience—and for those who want to maximize the magic—a private VIP tour is your ticket to the Disney day of your dreams. The red carpet is rolled out and you and your guests are the stars. "Let the concierge be your guide" as you explore the parks with a Disney expert, a highly trained tour guide who knows the ins and outs of the park, along with its history, fun facts, and trivia.

You call the shots, deciding where to go and when. Special requests are welcomed. If you're shopping and collecting souvenirs along the way, your guide can arrange for them to be delivered to your room. Other VIP tour benefits include hassle-free and customized planning, dining reservations, plus preferred parade and fireworks viewing. Expedited access to favorite attractions is also available for those eager to wait less and ride more.

At Walt Disney World, because of the sheer size of the resort, transportation from your resort hotel to all four parks (entering from backstage instead of the main gate) is included. If you are traveling with children, the appropriate size car seats will be installed in the van and will arrive with your tour guide.

VIP tours can be booked through Disney Special Activities one year in advance at Disneyland and 180 days in advance at Walt Disney World; they do not include theme park admission. Tours have a seven-hour minimum and are for 10 guests maximum, including infants. Variations of the VIP experience are available at other Disney parks in the world. ∎

During a VIP tour of Walt Disney World, your guide will meet you with a car—including car seats for little ones.

YOUR HAPPILY EVER AFTER

Say "I Do" to a Disney Fairy Tale Wedding

Ariel and Eric. Maid Marian and Robin Hood. Tiana and Naveen. Rapunzel and Flynn. You and your beloved. Disney Fairy Tale Weddings aren't just for characters in animated classics. Whatever you can imagine, envision, or wish for can become a dream come true.

Each Disney wedding venue is unique. Among the myriad of possibilities for theme park enthusiasts are the iconic castles, *Star Wars: Galaxy's Edge*, the Tree of Life, or the pavilions of EPCOT. Sail and say "I do" aboard a Disney cruise ship. Exchange leis at the tropical paradise that is Aulani, A Disney Resort & Spa. Transform a ballroom at a Disneyland or Walt Disney World resort into a weatherproof utopia. And, of course, there are the wedding gardens, from the intimate tucked into courtyards to the grandest of them all—Disney's Wedding Pavilion at Disney's Grand Floridian Resort & Spa. Along the shores of the Seven Seas Lagoon, the Wedding Pavilion sits on a private island among a lush garden oasis, truly a storybook setting. Victorian spires, vaulted ceilings, and an arched window behind the altar framing Cinderella Castle in the distance add to the romantic splendor.

Beyond the locations are the details for which Disney is famous. An episode of *Fairy Tale Weddings* on Disney+ highlighted the nuptials of Emily and John, a hockey-loving couple from Chicago. Although they helped plan everything from beginning to end, the Disney wedding specialists secretly

HAPPILY EVER AFTER

"Each happy ending's a brand-new beginning." —from the song "Ever Ever After" in *Enchanted* (2007)

OPPOSITE: Fairy tales do come true with a Walt Disney World dream wedding.

PAGES 382-3: Weddings at Walt Disney World can include the ultimate Disney princess experience: a ride in Cinderella's horse-drawn carriage.

arranged to surprise them with *the* Stanley Cup—the one that their favorite team won several times—as the centerpiece of their reception.

Arriving in style is a wedding statement unto itself. What's your fancy? Boat, Monorail, Segway, vintage Rolls-Royce? Regal horse-drawn landau coach like those used by royalty? Or perhaps the most popular of all—Cinderella's Coach, pulled by six Dapper Dan ponies, complete with white-wigged footmen, sparkling illumination, rich cerulean blue cushions, embossed gold leaf, two birds atop the carriage, and Suzy Mouse bringing up the rear.

Because this is a Fairy Tale Wedding, how about a cake that only Disney can do? Imagine telling your story on your wedding cake and bringing it to life with projection mapping technology! The images you choose are projected onto the blank canvas of the cake, coming alive in colorful and enchanting animation (just like the castles do during fireworks). And don't worry—it's all edible.

SAY YES TO THE DRESS

It's your big day. Which Disney princess would you like to emulate? The Disney Fairy Tale Weddings collection by Allure Bridals offers a collection of gowns inspired by the spirit, style, and stories of your favorite Disney princesses. The Pocahontas-themed gown features a lace overlay with a delicate pattern reminiscent of wind-swept autumn leaves. Suggestive of the ocean's current, Ariel's dress has tulle and organza swirls in a classic mermaid style. Belle, Aurora, Jasmine, Snow White, Tiana, Rapunzel, and Cinderella are represented, too.

OPPOSITE: Wedding cakes come as part of your Disney wedding package, themed to your favorite Disney film or character.

ABOVE: Pick your wedding backdrop, including a glowing Everest as you say "I do" at Disney's Animal Kingdom.

You choose the flavor and the fillings, while your interactive story becomes the "frosting" on top.

Still looking to "plus"—Disney speak to make it even better—your special day? Arrange appearances by your favorite Disney characters. Mickey and Minnie have been known to stand in as best man and maid of honor. Dazzle with a private fireworks display. Keep your guests entertained at the reception with the improvisational comedy of the "Tacky Tourists" and "Uninvited Wedding Guests." Photo opportunities don't have to be limited to the wedding venue. Arrange shots in front of Cinderella Castle, the Tree of Life, Spaceship Earth, or the Haunted Mansion. No request is too big or too small.

However you choose to say "I do," Disney Fairy Tale Weddings promises a magical celebration that is uniquely yours. ■

DINE LIKE A DISNEY

Degustation for Twelve

I n the 1960s, Walt was planning a second apartment above the Pirates of the Caribbean attraction (the first was located above the fire station). He planned to share it with his brother Roy. The gold *W* and *R* can still be seen in the wrought-iron veranda above the attraction. After Walt passed away, construction for the Disney family residence in New Orleans Square was never completed. Later, however, the space was repurposed for The Disney Gallery, a store showcasing Disney art and artifacts.

Introduced in 2008 as one of the Disney Dreams Giveaways during the Year of a Million Dreams and using concept art Walt commissioned from Disney Legend Dorothea Redmond, the Disneyland Dream Suite was built to reflect what Walt and his wife, Lilly, had envisioned. There is an all-new enchanted experience named for this exclusive location—21 Royal—and you and your guests are invited to dine in utmost Disney elegance.

Your evening begins on the patio with cocktails presented by the butler. Next, walk through the rooms and discover their magical and surprising features. Then it's time for the culinary adventure to begin. The stage is set at a lavish table in the Disney dining room, replete with white linens, gold-plated dinnerware, and fine crystal. Rivaling the experience at Michelin-starred restaurants, the multicourse tasting menu is prepared with the best of the best ingredients, perfectly plated, and presented with sophisticated flair. Dessert is served on the private balcony, with stunning views of the Rivers of America and prime viewing of the park's nighttime entertainment (including fireworks when offered). This is an unforgettable epicurean experience that is uniquely Disney! ∎

Have a dinner party in the heart of Disneyland. The table is set in the private residence envisioned by Walt and Lillian Disney.

ANTARCTICA TWO WAYS

Travel to the Most Remote Location on Earth

Discover Antarctica and wonders of nature that few people see. National Geographic Expeditions and Adventures by Disney each offer vacations to this remote destination, and both include experts who accompany you on the journey. How will you choose to encounter this otherworldly place close up?

Adventures by Disney launches its family-friendly expedition at the "end of the world"—Patagonia in South America. Begin your adventure in Buenos Aires. Then, with Disney-trained adventure guides and a team of naturalists, explore Tierra del Fuego, a national park that encompasses 160,000 acres (64,750 ha) of stunning natural landscapes ranging from lush forests and crystal clear lakes to rugged mountains and beautiful beaches. Don't miss a private ride on the End of the World Train on the world's southernmost functioning railway. Later, board the cruise ship and settle into your home for the next 10 days. Highlights include the Drake Passage—a legendary waterway coveted by seafaring adventurers. When you arrive in the Antarctic Peninsula, there are several excursions to consider, including an up close experience with a towering iceberg and a walk among penguin colonies. Don't miss the opportunity to take a Zodiac boat to a place few have gone before—Antarctica. Step foot on the seventh continent and explore terrain that is unlike any place on Earth!

With National Geographic Expeditions, experience Antarctica from every perspective while traveling with a team of scientists aboard the state-of-the-art *National Geographic Explorer, National Geographic Resolution,* or *National Geographic Endurance*—all Lindblad ships purposely built for polar

OPPOSITE: Zodiac boats get guests up close to towering icebergs and glaciers.

PAGES 390-91: On an Adventures by Disney tour of Antarctica, you'll walk on the seventh continent and see its penguin colonies.

expeditions. After convening and acclimating in Buenos Aires for two days, fly to Ushuaia, Argentina, the southernmost city in the world. Take a catamaran cruise on the scenic Beagle Channel before embarking the ship. While crossing the Drake Passage, enjoy talks from naturalists about the wildlife and geology that await on the Antarctic Peninsula. Once there, National Geographic keeps a flexible schedule, adapting the course to the conditions and opportunities that arise, such as observing a pod of orcas, walking a beach inhabited by seals and penguins, or kayaking amid brash ice. Other highlights include observing undersea specialists as they capture images of hardy marine life beneath the ice using a remotely operated vehicle (ROV). Plus, learn about the behaviors and interactions of different species, the geological and climatic forces that shape Antarctica, the anatomy of a glacier, and, this being National Geographic, how to take beautiful photographs! ■

ICEBREAKERS

Here are a few fun facts to start the conversation with your fellow adventurers: At the South Pole, *everywhere* you look is north. Don't let the ice fool you—Antarctica is a desert and one of the driest continents on Earth. There is no Antarctic time zone, nor are there trees or shrubs in Antarctica. Several species of polar fish have a special protein in their blood that is akin to antifreeze.

ADVENTURE INDEX

ACKNOWLEDGMENTS

When I was researching *Walt's Disneyland: A Walk in the Park with Walt Disney,* among the myriad of sources, the August 1963 issue of *National Geographic* magazine proved instrumental. Not just for the in-depth interview with Walt but also for one of the color photographs by Thomas Nebbia included in the issue: Walt joyfully signing autographs on Main Street, U.S.A. I chose the poignant image of Walt beaming in his beloved Disneyland as the cover of my book. Little did I know, that would be the beginning of my relationship with National Geographic.

In July 2021, Wendy Lefkon, my friend and Disney Editions editor, called explaining that National Geographic, now a part of the Disney family, was planning a book to celebrate The Walt Disney Company's 100th anniversary. Eager for me to consider the assignment, she introduced me to Allyson Johnson, senior editor for National Geographic, who then offered me this amazing project.

Allyson, thank you for trusting me with this tome. Your insight, enthusiasm, and patience are priceless. Our collaboration has been an adventure of a lifetime!

For Lisa Thomas and Lisa Gerry—aka Lisa T. and Lisa G.—I especially appreciate your sage suggestions and helpful navigation during the early stages of this book. Others at Nat Geo who made this book possible and to whom I express gratitude: Ashley Leath, Nicole M. Roberts, Elisa Gibson, Michael O'Connor, and Becca Saltzman. For the stunning imagery, Adrian Coakley. Copy editor Heather McElwain and proofreaders Jenny Miyasaki and Larry Shea. For the whimsical maps, Sara Mulvanny.

Thanks also to Chris Ostrander and his Synergy team, Cayla Ward, Linda Affhalter, and Steve Wilcox, for their incredible support researching this project at Walt Disney World. Also at the Most Magical Place on Earth: Kyle M. Huetter with Disney's Animals, Science and Environment program and VIP Guide Chris Girolamo. Friends in my Disney world who assisted: Mike Vargo, Kaye Malins, Caitlin Moneypenny-Johnston,

Bri Bertolaccini, Jeff Ino, Maria Massad, Amber Washington, Sammy Ferzacca, Ryan March, Christoph Zbinden, and Joseph Titizian.

Joe Rohde, my first wish was for you to write the foreword, and my dream came true. Namaste! Jen Eastwood, I appreciate your advising and guiding the editors of this book. Kevin M. Kern, Nicole M. Carroll, Ed Ovalle, and Mike Buckhoff in the Walt Disney Archives, always an honor and pleasure to work with you.

For everyone at The Walt Disney Company who contributed and assisted, my sincere gratitude.

Lastly, to Tom Sawyer and Huck Finn, who first taught me what adventure is . . .

ABOUT THE AUTHORS

MARCY CARRIKER SMOTHERS is the author of the fan favorite *Eat Like Walt: The Wonderful World of Disney Food,* a *New York Times* New & Noteworthy selection. A noted radio personality, she has hosted several programs, including *The Food Guy and Marcy Show* with Food Network's Guy Fieri. In celebration of the 50th anniversary of Walt Disney World, she co-authored *Delicious Disney: Walt Disney World: Recipes & Stories From the Most Magical Place on Earth.* Her love of all things Disney—especially Disneyland—inspired her to write *Walt's Disneyland: A Walk in the Park With Walt Disney.*

JOE ROHDE (foreword) spent more than 40 years as an Imagineer for The Walt Disney Company, bringing to life some of Disney's most iconic experiences and attractions, including Disney's Animal Kingdom Theme Park; Aulani, A Disney Resort & Spa; and most recently, Pandora—The World of Avatar. An artist, conservationist, traveler, and storyteller, he now works as a creative consultant.

ILLUSTRATIONS CREDITS

PHOTOS FROM THE WALT DISNEY COMPANY (TWDC)
Cover, Photo illustration by Matt Stroshane; back cover, Andrea Barnett; 2-3, Kent Phillips; 4-5, Jeff Clausen/Mark Stockbridge; 7, TWDC; 9, TWDC Archives; 13(B/C), TWDC Archives; 14, TWDC Archives; 15(C/D), TWDC Archives; 17(C/E), TWDC Archives; 18-9, Matt Stroshane; 22-3, Justin Seeley; 24, Kent Phillips; 27, TWDC; 28-30, Matt Stroshane; 31, Ryan Wendler; 33, TWDC; 35, David Roark; 36-7, Gary Copeland; 38(A), Andrea Barnett; 38(D), TWDC; 39(B), Kent Phillips; 39(C), Kim Ruggiero; 39(E/H), Ali Nasser; 39(F), Chloe Rice; 39(G), David Roark; 40-1, Kent Phillips; 43, TWDC; 46(A), Amy Smith; 47(E/F/G/H), TWDC Archives; 51, Kent Phillips; 53-7, TWDC; 62-3, Chris Sista; 65, Caitie McCabe; 66-9, Kent Phillips; 71-4(A/D), Matt Stroshane; 75(B/E), Chloe Rice; 75(C), David Roark; 75(F), TWDC; 75(G), Kent Phillips; 75(H), Todd Anderson; 77-81, TWDC; 83, Chloe Rice; 88-9, Chloe Rice; 91, David Nguyen; 92-3, Kent Phillips; 94(A), Andrea Barnett; 94(D), Mark Ashman; 95(B), Caitie McCabe; 95(C/F), Preston Mack; 95(E), Chloe Rice; 95(G), Ali Nasser; 95(H), Ryan Wendler; 97, Chloe Rice; 99-101, Matt Stroshane; 102, Chloe Rice; 103, Amy Smith; 105, Diana Zalucky; 106-7, Andrea Barnett; 109-11, Kent Phillips; 112, Bob Desmond; 113, Matt Stroshane; 114(A), Andrea Barnett; 114(D), David Roark; 115(B), Jeff Nickel; 115(C), David Roark; 115(E), Kent Phillips; 115(F), Andrea Barnett; 115(G/H), Bob Desmond; 117, Florian Geis; 119-23(A/B/D/G/H), TWDC; 123(C/E/F), Chloe Rice; 124-5, Bob Desmond; 127, Preston Mack; 130-1, TWDC Archives; 133-5, Caitie McCabe; 136-7, Charlie Champagne; 139, TWDC; 141, Diana Zalucky; 143, Chloe Rice; 145, Kent Phillips; 146-7, Matt Stroshane; 149, Steven Diaz; 151, Kent Phillips; 152-3, TWDC; 154-5, David Roark; 157-9, TWDC Archives; 161, Matt Stroshane; 163, TWDC; 164-5, Preston Mack; 167, Chris Sista; 168-9, Chloe Rice; 171, Claire and Jeremy Weiss; 173, Matt Stroshane; 174-5, David Roark; 176, TWDC; 177, Chris Sista; 178-9, Matt Stroshane; 181, Diana Zalucky; 182-3, Ryan Wendler; 189, Kent Phillips; 193-5, TWDC Archives; 198-200, Chloe Rice; 201, TWDC; 203, Matt Stroshane; 204-6(A), Caitie McCabe; 206(D), Matt Stroshane; 207(B), Jeff Nickel; 207(C/E/G), Caitie McCabe; 207(F), Frédéric Lagrange; 207(H), Matt Stroshane; 214-7, Matt Stroshane; 219, Diana Zalucky; 221, Todd Anderson; 222-3, Jeff Clausen/Mark Stockbridge; 224(D), Jeff Clausen/Mark Stockbridge; 225(B/E), Jeff Clausen/Mark Stockbridge; 225(C), Bob Desmond; 225(F), Todd Anderson; 225(G), David Roark; 227, Kent Phillips; 230, Kent Phillips; 233-5, TWDC Archives; 240-1, Kent Phillips; 246, TWDC; 248-53, TWDC; 255, Kent Phillips; 259, Photo illustration by Kent Phillips; 260-1, Jeff Clausen; 263, Mark Stockbridge; 264-5, Matt Stroshane; 267, David Roark; 269, Diana Zalucky; 270-2(A), Kent Phillips; 272(D), Caitie McCabe; 273(B), Chloe Rice; 273(C/E/H), Caitie McCabe; 273(F), Melanie Acevedo; 273(G), Amy Smith; 275, Matt Stroshane; 276-7, Chris Sista; 278-9, Matt Stroshane; 287, David Nguyen; 289, Kent Phillips; 290-1, Jeff Clausen; 293, Kent Phillips; 295-7, Scott Watt; 299, Wes Lagattolla; 300-1, David Mau; 303, Matt Stroshane; 304-5, TWDC; 307-9, Jeff Clausen/Mark

Stockbridge; 311, Kent Phillips; 313, Chloe Rice; 315, Ali Nasser; 316-7, TWDC; 318, Johnny Castle; 319, David Nguyen; 320(A/D), TWDC; 321(B), Jimmy DeFlippo; 321(C), Chloe Rice; 321(E), David Nguyen; 321(F), TWDC; 321(G), Gene Duncan; 321(H), Charlene Guilliams; 322(A), Debi Harbin; 322(B), Kelsey Noland; 322(E), Ali Nasser; 322(F/G), David Nguyen; 322(H), Kent Phillips; 323(C), Kent Phillips; 323(D), TWDC; 323(I), Kelsey Noland; 323(J), Matt Stroshane; 325, TWDC; 327, Kent Phillips; 329, Jimmy DeFlippo; 331, Kent Phillips; 332-3, TWDC; 335, Jimmy Marble; 336-7, Gary Copeland; 340-1, Kent Phillips; 347, Chloe Rice; 348-9, TWDC Archives; 350(A/D), Chloe Rice; 351(B), TWDC; 351(C/F), Bob Desmond; 351(E), Jeff Nickel; 351(G), Kent Phillips; 351(H), Diana Zalucky; 352-3, Matt Stroshane; 355, Wes Lagattolla; 356(A/D), Kent Phillips; 357(B), Matt Stroshane; 357(C), Amy Smith; 357(E/G/H), Kent Phillips; 357(F), David Roark; 359, TWDC; 360(A), Andrea Barnett; 360(D), Gene Duncan; 361(B/C/E/G/H), Gene Duncan; 361(F), Matt Stroshane; 363, Jeff Clausen/Mark Stockbridge; 364-5, Steve Carsella; 369, Matt Stroshane; 370(A/D), Chloe Rice; 371(B), Preston Mack; 371(C/E/G/H), Wes Lagattolla; 371(F), David Roark; 373, TWDC Archives; 374-5, Jeff Clausen/Mark Stockbridge; 379, Chloe Rice; 381, Claire Celeste; 382-3, Diana Zalucky; 384, Meredith Filip; 385, Claire Celeste; 387, Matt Stroshane; 389-91, Chloe Rice; Gatefold: Bob Desmond (Golden Horseshoe/Guest Book/The *Mark Twain*); Cicilia Teng (Exercise); Russell Kirk (Fore Fun); Caitie McCabe (Disney Story); Abigail F. Nilsson (Sangria University); Jimmy DeFlippo (I Think I Can); Chloe Rice (Animal Signs/Ultimate Easter Egg); Matt Stroshane (World's Fair); TWDC (Arendelle/Three-Dream Circus); Kent Phillips (Dino Day/Hideouts/Kungaloosh); David Roark (A Global Affair); Tony Grable (Pack Your Capes).

PHOTOS FROM OTHER SOURCES

10-11, Tom Nebbia/Corbis via Getty Images; 12, Clement Philippe/Arterra/Alamy Stock Photo (Alamy); 13(D), Max/Alamy; 15(B), Sorin Colac/Alamy; 16(A), Moritz Wolf/imageBROKER/Alamy; 16(B), Michael Runkel/robert harding/Alamy; 17(D), Adam Eastland/Alamy; 21, Stephen Searle/Alamy; 25, Disney Magic/Alamy; 45, Daisy-Photography/Alamy; 46(LE), ItzaVU/Shutterstock; 46(D), AugustSnow/Alamy; 47(B), Helen Sessions/Alamy; 47(C), Sunshine/Alamy; 49, Jeff Gritchen/Digital First Media/Orange County Register via Getty Images; 59, Sundry Photography/Alamy; 60-1, Courtesy of The Walt Disney Family Museum; 85, Bill Grant/Alamy; 86-7, USC Libraries/Corbis via Getty Images; 129, Logan Bush/Shutterstock; 185, Andrew Coleman/National Geographic Image Collection; 186-7, Angus McComiskey/Alamy; 190-1, Artur Maltsau/Alamy; 197, Henryk Sadura/Alamy; 209, Konrad Wothe/Image Professionals GmbH/Alamy; 210-1, Ralph Lee Hopkins; 212, Andrew Peacock/Getty Images; 213, Timothy Mulholland/Alamy; 224(A), Janos Rautonen/Alamy; 225(H), Brandon Cole/ Alamy; 228-9, Marshall Ikonography/Alamy; 231, Noppasin Wongchum/Alamy; 237, Tom Murphy/National Geographic Image Collection; 238-9, Moose Henderson/Shutterstock; 243, Jan Wlodarczyk/Alamy; 244-5, Alexandr Ozerov/Alamy; 247, Nordic Images/Alamy; 256-7, Alan Copson/roberthardin-g; 281, Myung J. Chun/LA Times via Getty Images; 282-3, Sarah Hadley/Alamy; 284, Brian Kinney/Alamy; 285, Logan Bush/Shutterstock; 339, SIPA Asia via ZUMA Press Wire/Alamy; 342-3, Parinya Suwanitch/Alamy; 345, Nice-Prospects-Prime/Alamy; 367, Ricardo Ramirez Buxeda/Orlando Sentinel/TNS/Alamy; 376-7, National Geographic Expeditions; Gatefold: Sunshine Pics/Alamy (Starstruck); Alan Copson/JAI/Alamy (Route 66); Blaize Pascall/Alamy (Get Curiouser); Robert Fried/Alamy (Silverado Trail); Joni Hanebutt/Alamy (Club Cool).

Since 1888, the National Geographic Society has funded more than 14,000 research, conservation, education, and storytelling projects around the world. National Geographic Partners distributes a portion of the funds it receives from your purchase to National Geographic Society to support programs including the conservation of animals and their habitats.

Get closer to National Geographic Explorers and photographers, and connect with our global community. Join us today at nationalgeographic.org/joinus

For rights or permissions inquiries, please contact National Geographic Books Subsidiary Rights: bookrights@natgeo.com

ISBN: 978-1-4262-2264-1 (trade)

ISBN: 978-1-4262-2280-1 (deluxe)

The information in this book has been carefully checked and to the best of our knowledge is accurate. However, details are subject to change, and the publisher cannot be responsible for such changes, or for errors or omissions. Assessments of sites, hotels, and restaurants are based on the author's subjective opinions, which do not necessarily reflect the publisher's opinion.

Some images shown throughout this publication do not represent current operational guidelines or health and safety measures such as face covering and physical distancing requirements. Visit https://disneyworld.disney.go.com for important details to know before you visit.

Printed in the United States of America

22/WOR/1